THE WCC
Iliad of Homer

— Translated abridged and annotated —

contact@wexyork.com

Maps of the Classics

Not so long ago, well-educated people could read classic literary texts in their original language. Today it is possible to teach in a university without being able to read any language other than your own. WexYork Compact Classics have been prepared to offer classic texts in abridged and translated form along with brief introductions and basic notes — nothing too scholarly and specialised. They are not versions, adaptations or re-workings of their originals: simply guides bearing the same sort of relationship to texts that maps do to the territory they describe, in no way replacing them.

Introduction

The *Iliad* is the West's earliest epic: that is, a long poetic story of great achievements centred around a great hero. In this case the story is that of an ancient feud between a federation of Greek tribes and the Asian city of Troy in over a thousand years BC. It is, then, a story of violence in which the deaths of men are described in often horrific detail. But there is no gloating over pain and hardship, and so far from being depressed or depressing, the *Iliad* has in all its 2700 years thrilled readers as moving, exciting and life-affirming. Human existence, it maintains, can be noble, fulfilling and worthwhile in spite of its brevity and pain. In fact Homer's immortal gods, for whom all that happens on earth appears as an interesting game at best, seem almost to envy man's capacity to suffer and die since, as a result, he is able to dare, dream, exult and live life on the edge.

oooOooo

Written around 750 BC, the *Iliad* comprises some 16,000 lines of highly formalised verse here presented in English prose summary that cannot avoid missing its original's brilliance and power. The Trojan War lasted ten years, Homer tells us, but he covers events only in its final year. It resulted from the theft of a woman – Helen of Troy — from Menelaus, one of the Greek federation chiefs, by the Trojan hero Paris. In fact other explanations have been proposed at various times, but really it hardly matters. War was a condition of life in which men were either remembered or forgotten, depending on how greatly and gloriously they lived and died. That was what mattered.

oooOooo

As in the war as a whole, conflict in the *Iliad* stems from the theft of a woman, in this case, one possessed by Achilles, the Greeks' greatest fighter, but claimed by Agamemnon, the Greek commander-in-chief. Homer's assertion in his opening lines that his subject is the resulting anger of Achilles is misleading, though, for in fact Achilles sulks in retirement, returning to the action only in the last quarter of the epic when his comrade Patroclus is killed by the Trojan Hector whom he in turn kills. The story then ends with Hector's funeral, the war not yet over.

Without the irresistible Achilles, the action comprises the deeds of other Greek heroes along with episodes such as a night raid on the encamped Trojans by Ulysses and Diomedes. One of its most striking features though is its many unexpected excursions into other events and stories. In Book 6, for example, the Greek hero Diomedes and Trojan Glaucus meet and prepare to fight — but no blow-by-blow account of their duel follows. In fact the two introduce themselves — as the result of which they learn that their families are long-standing friends. The excursion includes a history of the mythical Greek hero Bellerophon over the course of some hundred lines, as the result of which Diomedes and Glaucus decide not to fight after all but exchange armour instead!

This story within a story is not an irrelevance. In the early heroic age, families and individuals mattered, not states, safety and protection being made possible by friendships and alliances cemented by gifts and hospitality. Homeric heroes generally knew each other, but where they did not, it paid, as here, to check the history of whoever you considered fighting. Glaucus and Diomedes are a reminder that the Trojan War itself resulted from an abuse of hospitality when the Trojan Paris stole Helen, a Greek chief's wife while staying under his roof.

In probably the most famous of these 'excursions', near the end, the blacksmith-god Hephaestus forges armour to replace that stripped by Hector from the dead body of Patroclus (a standard heroic battle prize), engraving it with earth and stars, weddings and festivals and the countryside rituals of farming, harvest-home and dancing. Its 146 lines heighten hold up the action but remind readers that however violent and destructive the war, somewhere or other the peaceful business of life went on. The 20th Century poet W H Auden's version of this incident in his poem *The Shield of Achilles*, read by him, can be heard in an online British Library Sound Archive recording.

oooOooo

The brilliance of Homer's verse cannot be described, much less imitated, in English prose summary, but one well-known feature needs comment since even in translation it stands out. Similes may express similarity, but Homer's are often startlingly unexpected. In one famous one, a fighter dies on his feet, hit by a javelin, his head falling forward like a flower nodding on its stalk. Sometimes extended comparisons make long excursions in themselves. In my personal favourite, in the deafening uproar and heat of a Trojan attack on the Greek ships, a sky filled with arrows, rocks and javelins is compared to a blizzard on some lonely winter coast, its first distant flurries whitening out mountains, then nearer fields, farms and hamlets, finally blanketing the shingle and drawn-up boats on the beach with its whirling flakes, hushing and immobilising nature. Then, with a bang we are suddenly back in deafening conflict that is more like a high-speed multiple car smash than any battle we can imagine.

oooOooo

The *Iliad* falls into twenty-four books because each "book" held what could be contained on a single papyrus scroll, and the story is certainly not original in our modern sense, being composed and written down from memorised verse stories chanted to a lute accompaniment by bards at feasts and on ceremonial occasions. Homer's hearers clearly remembered this tradition, for such chanting bards crop up in the epic. When Odysseus and other heroes call on Achilles to take away the woman Agamemnon claims from him, they find him "playing his lyre and singing of the heroic deeds of men" to his doomed second-in-command Patroclus.

You may, by the way, have forgotten by now who Agamemnon was, for one of the problems Homer gives us is his huge cast of men, women, gods and events, all known and familiar to his hearers and often only briefly referred to in passing but unknown to most modern readers. To help out, in addition to very occasional footnotes to clarify important puzzles without interrupting the story, there is a summary index at the beginning and, at the end, a glossary of "Gods, heroes and others" for you to consult.

Summary Index

bury their dead, while the Greeks also build a defensive wall round their ships.

Zeus prompts a Trojan counter-offensive that drives the Greeks back to their ships. The Trojans camp outside the Greeks' new wall.

In council, Agamemnon proposes flight, but the other Greek heroes send a deputation to Achilles instead, hoping to persuade him to rejoin them. They fail in spite of Agamemnon's offer of huge compensation but resolve to fight on anyway.

That night, Diomedes and Odysseus go on a scouting expedition, capture a Trojan spy and attack a camp of newly-arrived Thracians, killing their chief Rhesus and stealing his horses and chariot.

Next day, Agamemnon leads a Greek attack that forces the Trojans back into their city. But then the Trojans counter-attack, driving the Greeks back to their ships. Nestor urges Patroclus to lead Achilles' troops himself in order to save the expedition.

The Trojans storm the Greek protecting wall and attack the ships.

Now Cretan Idomeneus, a Greek ally, goes on the heroic rampage, killing many Trojans.

The god Poseidon helps the Greeks while Zeus sleeps, and battle sways the Greeks' way again.

Zeus wakes and forbids Poseidon to interfere further, with the result that the Greeks are pushed back to their ships once more. Hector actually fires one ship.

Achilles lends Patroclus his armour. Patroclus goes on his own heroic rampage, killing large numbers of Trojans and almost storming Troy before himself being killed by Hector.

Book 1

Sing, goddess,[1] the story of Achilles' anger that cost so many lives and so much grief. What god set him and Agamemnon at each other's throats?

It was Apollo who sent disease raging through the army when ransom was refused for the daughter of his priest Chryses. The old man pleaded with Agamemnon for the return of his daughter, but Agamemnon would not listen, so he prayed to the god instead – who did. Down came Apollo with his silver bow and plague arrows. First he killed the animals, then the men. Everywhere corpse fires burnt until, on the tenth day, Achilles called a council at which the Greeks' seer Calchas,[2] who knew all about birds and omens, spoke – first asking Achilles for protection in case anything he said offended Agamemnon.

"Speak freely," Achilles told him, so Calchas gave his judgement, which was that Apollo had sent the plague and

---

[1]

Calliope, muse of epic poetry, one of the nine muse-daughters of Mnemosyne, goddess of memory. The illiterate bards of the old stories Homer based himself on had to memorise everything and so appealed directly to her at the start!

[2]

Divination of the events and the future, mostly by studying entrails and the flight of birds. Nothing of importance was done without it.

would continue loosing off his arrows of disease until they sacrificed to him and return Chryseis to her father.

Next Agamemnon stood up, his heart thudding with anger. "Calchas, I never yet heard you say anything anyone wanted to hear. The girl pleases me. In fact I like her better than my wife. For the army's sake I will give her up if she really is the cause of our suffering — but only if I am awarded some other prize to make up for her.

"Greedy as always," Achilles jeered. "Who else is there we can give you in exchange? Everything is shared out already, and it would be wrong to take back from others what has already been awarded."

"You think it right that I should give up my prize but not you, do you? Do not give me orders, Achilles. Either the Greeks award me another woman or I will take one – from you if necessary. Still, all that can wait. Let a ship be hauled down to the water[3] and crewed so that one of you can return Chryseis to her father and reconcile us to great Apollo."

Now though Achilles was angry too. "Why should I, or anyone, obey your orders?" he asked. "The Trojans never harmed me or stole anything of mine. I am only here at all for your sake, and now you threaten to strip me of my prize. I have had enough. I am going home."

"Go on, then – run away," the army commander jeered back. "I will not miss you, and you were always a trouble-maker. Before you go though and so that nobody here can doubt

----

[3]

Homeric ships are small enough to be dragged about, more like Viking longboats than the triremes of later centuries.

14

which of us is greater, I declare that I will take your Briseis to compensate for my loss."

Achilles was on the point of drawing his sword and killing the man where he stood, but Athene appeared out of the sky in the nick of time, visible only to him and pulling him back by the hair.[4]

"Be ruled by me," the grey-eyed goddess urged. "Hera has sent me. She loves you as I do and promises that what you lose now will be made up to you three-fold."

"Goddess," Achilles answered her after a pause, "angry as I am, I will obey you, for when men listen to the gods, the gods are more likely to listen to them."

So he pushed his sword back in its scabbard and turned to the commander-in-chief again. "Agamemnon, you are a fool and a coward. Now listen to what *I* swear. This staff in my hand[5] will sooner sprout leaves than hear me break my word: the day will come when the Greeks will drop in their crowds before man-killing Hector — and then you will eat your hearts out for dishonouring me."

He threw down the staff studded with golden nails as wise old Nestor spoke up, two generations older than either of them and fond of both.

---

[4]

Homer's gods are often sometimes personifications of human attributes as well as divine powers. Athene, for example, is associated with prudence and wisdom as was Aphrodite with sex and desire.

[5]

In formal public debates, a staff is passed to the speaker who then hands it on, the aim being to avoid interruptions and fights.

"If only the Trojans could see you two now, how pleased they would be." he said. "In my time I have known men greater and stronger than either of you, yet they always listened to me, and so will you if you have any sense. Agamemnon, you have no business taking another man's prize. Achilles, you have no business putting yourself on equal footing with our commander. You are both in the wrong. Both of you, then, give way in this quarrel."

"Your words are wise, sir," Agamemnon answered, "but I will not put up with this man's insults."

'You think you can insult me while I must not insult you and do whatever you say?" Achilles retorted. "Very well, take my prize. I will not fight over what you yourself awarded – but tell your men to touch nothing else of mine or you will find yourself on the end of my spear."

So the assembly broke up. Achilles stormed off to his tents while men hauled a ship down to the water and Agamemnon detailed a crew of twenty men and stowed animals aboard for the sacrifice. Then he appointed Talthybius and Eurybates to fetch the girl Briseis and these left reluctantly on their mission.

Achilles saw them approach. "Welcome, heralds," he greeted them graciously. "Don't be afraid. I know this business is none of your making. Patroclus, fetch the Trojan girl."

So his friend fetched Briseis, who left their tents unwillingly. Later, though, alone by himself on the sea-shore, Achilles wept and prayed to his mother, calling out over the grey and empty sea.

"Mother, since I am not fated to enjoy long life, Zeus owes me honour in exchange, yet now I am dishonoured more than any man alive." At that his mother Thetis came out of the sea to weep with him and stroke his hand. "Mother," he ended, "Zeus owes you a debt, so beg him for me to grant glory to the

Trojans until Agamemnon is forced to admit that he wronged and dishonoured me."

"Child," mourned his mother, "born to a life as unhappy as it must be short, Zeus is away from Olympus and will not be back for twelve days. When he returns, though, I will ask him for what you want, and I think I may be able to persuade him."

While they were speaking, Odysseus and the others sailed to a cove where the priest Chryses was just then tending Apollo's altar. There he restored the girl to her father and prepared the sacrifice. The priest then prayed to the archer-god to lift his curse – which Apollo graciously did – while they scattered barley meal, killed and skinned the sacrificial animals, poured wine over the pieces of meat and roasted them.[6] Afterwards, they slept on the beach near their ship, and the next day the god sent a following wind for their return voyage, and so they landed on the wide, flat sea-plain and dragged their vessel up the beach once more. Meanwhile Achilles moped in his quarters, missing the fighting, but after twelve days Zeus returned to Olympus from the land of the Aethiopians and Thetis made her promised plea to him on her son's behalf.

The god who gathers the clouds listened and was silent for a long time. "What you ask will not please Hera who blames me for favouring the Trojans too much already," he answered, "but I will do what you say." He nodded his head to confirm his oath, at which all Olympus shook. So Thetis returned to

---

[6]
Standard ritual for prayers and sacrifice before feasts and on all ceremonial occasions.

her home in the sea while the other gods all greeted Zeus respectfully, except Hera.

"What are you plotting now?" she demanded. "you who always keep your thoughts to yourself and let no-one know what is in your mind."

"While you want always to know too much and ask questions about matters that do not concern you," the father of gods answered her. "Whatever is proper for you to know, I tell you. What is not, I keep to myself."

But Hera was not to be put down. "Why did you bow your head in assent to Thetis?" she persisted. " Did you promise to honour Achilles by letting the Trojans drive the Greeks back to their ships?"

"Always asking questions, always suspicious," Zeus grumbled, avoiding direct answer, "with the result that you only estrange me from you more than ever. Sit down and be quiet, for fear I lay my unconquerable hands on you."

So Hera sat down in fear while Hephaestus the smith-god hurried to comfort her. "Can there ever be pleasure in heaven if we immortals forever squabble over mortals?" he asked. "Mother, be gracious to Zeus who is stronger than any of us." He hobbled over to put the great two-handled drinking cup in her hands. "Once before I tried to protect you from him but only got thrown out of heaven by my foot and lamed for my pains. All day I hurtled earthwards, crashing only in the evening on the island of Lemnos."

His mother smiled in reply and accepted his offered nectar,[7] after which the smith-god hobbled about serving the others as well so that they all laughed and relaxed again.

And so they feasted and drank until the sun went down. Apollo played his harp, the muses sang, and all finally went up to sleep in the beautiful houses that the smith-god had built for them while Zeus himself enjoyed sweet sleep in his great bed with his wife Hera.

---

[7] Homer's gods enjoyed the smell of animal sacrifices but kept immortal body and soul together exclusively with ambrosia (what that was we don't know) and nectar.

Book 2

While men and gods slept, Zeus alone lay awake thinking about how best to bring honour to Achilles. At last he sent a dream to Agamemnon, filling him with thoughts of battle and deluding him into believing the gods were no longer divided about Troy's fate. The dream took in Agamemnon so completely that when dawn broke, he ordered his heralds to assemble the army. First, though, he held a council with his chiefs.

"Friends," he told them, "I dreamt last night that a god visited me in the guise of old Nestor here saying that Hera had persuaded the other Olympians to turn against Troy at last. We will attack then – only first I mean to test the army's morale by suggesting that we give up and go home. Your job will be to persuade them to stand firm if need be."

Nestor himself then rose to speak, remarking very deliberately that if anyone other than his commander-in-chief had described such a dream and proposed such a ruse, he would consider him stark mad. Still, he and the others left to carry out Agamemnon's wish, and soon the heralds had the army called to assembly in a gathering so huge that the earth itself shook under its weight. The god Hephaestus himself had made the sceptre given to Zeus who in turn gave it to Hermes from whom it descended to Agamemnon. The commander now wielded it to get his soldiers' attention.

"Soldiers," he cried, "I have been cheated by Zeus who promised me Troy but has since abandoned me so that now I have no choice but to sail home in disgrace, even though you, my fighting men, still outnumber the Trojans by at least ten to one. Nine years have passed since we arrived. Our ships' timbers have crumbled and rigging rotted. Our wives and children have missed us for too long. Let them wait no longer."

Then the assembly was shaken as though by a great storm, as when Zeus drives on a westerly gale through steep seas or nodding fields of wheat. The soldiers broke and ran pell-mell to the ships, snatching at the props holding them up as they arrived, making ready to drag them down to the sea's edge. At Hera's command, Athene then hurtled down from Olympus to Odysseus, urging him to rally the men and make them stand firm, and this the hero did, throwing off his cloak for his herald Eurybates to pick up as he hared around, grabbing Agamemnon's staff on his way to rally the men.

"Don't show yourselves to be fools as well as cowards," he roared to them. "Agamemnon was only testing your courage and loyalty – and heaven help you if you fail him." Then he spoke fiercely to the other chiefs. "You heard Agamemnon's plan. Do as he ordered. Persuade your men back to the assembly. Only one man's word can be law in an army."

In this way he calmed, heartened and ordered the men back to the assembly where only Thersites now spoke in favour of leaving. He was the Greeks' ugliest and most insubordinate trouble-maker: bandy-legged, lame in one foot, stooped, round-shouldered and with a pointy skull on which his fuzzy hair draggled thinly.

"Now what is it you want from us, Agamemnon?" this man screamed. "What more treasures do you need to add to the ones already bulging out the sides of your tents – won for you by *us*? I say we leave you here to fight your own battles since you dishonoured Achilles who is a greater man than you any day."

Odysseus moved quickly. "My, what a way with words you have, Thersites," he congratulated him. "Only face it, you are not in the same class as your betters and have no business bandying speeches with them. Try it again and I will send you back to the ships naked and howling."

At that he clouted the man so hard with the speaker's staff that he doubled up and started to cry, a great bloody welt opening up across his shoulders. At that everyone laughed happily. Nobody had much time for Thersites.

Odysseus waited for silence again before turning to the commander-in-chief. "Agamemnon, there are some snivellers here who would like to make a fool of you, forgetting the oath they swore when they left never to return home until Troy was sacked. Of course we feel sorry for them. Of course it is hard to be away so long from wife and home – but not so hard as it would be to make ourselves laughing-stocks by enduring so much without ever finding out if Calchas' prophesy was true or not when we stopped at Aulis on our way here and sacrificed by a spring in the shade of a plane tree. A great snake slithered into sight, climbed the tree and ate a hatch of eight sparrow nestlings in it — adding their mother, a ninth mouthful, as she fluttered about its head. You all saw the omen, and Calchas interpreted it to mean that we would have to fight nine years before taking Troy in the tenth. Surely, we are not going to give up now that we are so close to the promised time?"

Now the soldiers changed their tune and started to roar for war. Then old Nestor added his voice. "Of late we have been bandying too many words and throwing too few spears," he shouted. "Agamemnon, lead us into battle — after sending away any cowards who prefer an inglorious trip home instead. Then we will know the truth of that other omen, when lightning flashing out of the sky on our right as we set sail for Troy promising us good luck. We who stay here will go home only after bedding some Trojan's wife and grabbing huge plunder that will make all our pains worthwhile. In fact I suggest you sort out your soldiers into their original clans and tribes again so that we can see which are the best and most skilful in battle and which are not so good."

"As always, Nestor," answered Agamemnon, "you prove yourself the best of us in debate. If I had ten more counsellors like you, we could have taken Troy long ago. Still, I have made enough mistakes, none more serious that when I lost my temper with Achilles, so let every man now prepare for fighting by getting a good meal inside him, putting an edge to his spear and checking his gear over."

The answering shout from his soldiers was like the crash of storm surf against a cliff, and they all did as he ordered, eating their meal and praying to the gods while Agamemnon himself feasted his chieftains on a fat ox. Nestor was there, of course, as were also Idomeneus the Cretan, the two Ajaxes, Odysseus – cleverest by far of all the Greeks – and Menelaus who, as Agamemnon's, brother hardly needed an invitation. They all stood in a circle round the sacrificed beast as it was roasted, and when all had finished eating, their hunger satisfied, Nestor once more spoke.

"Now, Agamemnon, with bellies full and spirits high, now is the time to attack, before the men's ardour cools again."

So Agamemnon sent his heralds to summon the fighting men while his chieftains marshalled them into their divisions.

They came together like a migration of geese, cranes and swans, the flower-studded plain of the Scamander river shaking under the weight of their feet and horses' hooves. Agamemnon, prominent as a bull among heifers, reviewed them there, so tell me, Muse, for you know everything that ever happened on this earth – what were the forces of the Greeks and the numbers of their ships?[8]

First came the Boeotians who arrived in fifty ships holding a hundred and twenty men each. Then came men from Aspledon and Orchomenos in a squadron of thirty vessels. Fighting alongside the Boeotians came men of Phocis in forty ships. Ajax the son of Oïleus commanded forty Locrian ships from across the straits facing Euboea. This Ajax might have been smaller than his giant namesake Telamonian Ajax but had no equal as a spear-thrower. Euboea itself sent forty ships with men who wore their hair long and carried ash spears.

Next, in fifty ships, came the Athenians beside whom the greater Telamonian Ajax from Salamis had beached his twelve ships. Diomedes of the great war-cry with two other chiefs led men from Argos, Tiryns, vine-rich Epidaurus and other cities in eighty ships. In a hundred more ships came men from Mycenae, Corinth and many neighbouring cities, all led by

---

[8]

In this, the 'Catalogue of Ships', vessels are enumerated rather than men, as soldiers in later wars might be enumerated by regiments since it is easier to count in large units. Trojans, though, are presented just as tribes with named leaders. The Catalogue was important because the *Iliad* was recited at festivals for people who considered themselves descendants of those who fought at Troy. For brevity, many names and details are omitted here from the lists.

Agamemnon himself, and in sixty ships came men of Lacedaemon led by his brother Menelaus.

Next, from Pylos and the lovely countryside around came ninety ships commanded by old Nestor. There were Arcadians from the region around Mount Cyllene in sixty ships lent by Agamemnon since these inlanders knew nothing of sea-faring. Then came Men from Buprasion and much of Elis in ten ships.

From Dulichium and other islands off Elis came men in forty ships. Odysseus led the men of Ithaka and its more northerly islands in twelve ships with crimson painted bows, then the Aetolians in forty more.

In eighty ships came Idomeneus and Meriones leading fighters from Crete of the hundred towns, while from Rhodes came nine shiploads led by Tlepolemus, Heracles' tall and handsome son. Next came Nireus, handsomest of all the Greeks at Troy except Achilles – only, unlike him, a weakling with only three ships.

Achilles himself had brought fifty shiploads from Argos, although these were not now in the line of battle, having been stood down by their chief who was still sick at heart, missing the gentle girl Briseis.

From Phylace and the lands round about came men led first by Protesilaus. He, though, among the first to leap ashore at Troy, had been killed first as well, so his followers in their forty ships were now led by his younger brother. Men from around Pherae came in eleven ships, archers from Methone, Thaumace, Meliboea and Olizon in fifty ships led by Philoctetes, greatest archer of them all. He being sick of snake-bite on the isle of Lemnos, though, his men were now led by Medon.

There were men from Tricce, Ithome and Oechalia in thirty ships, forty shiploads more from Ormenion, Asterion and

Titanus. From Argissa and thereabouts came forty boatloads and finally Enienes and Peraebians in twenty-two ships while Prothous commanded the Magnetes in another forty.

These were the Greek contingents. Admetus had by far the best horses – matched mares reared by Apollo of The Silver Bow himself in Peraea – while best of the men by far after Achilles was Telamonian Ajax. Now the earth itself shuddered under their feet as news of their approach was carried to the Trojans by Iris of the whirlwind feet disguised as Priam's son Polites who had been posted as look-out.

"Father," said the disguised goddess to Priam who was then in conference with other Trojans, "the enemy is marching towards us in numbers like those of forest leaves or sands of the sea. Hector, we have allies who speak in different languages, so take my advice and deploy them in separate troops led by their own captains."

So the Trojans too rushed to arms, forming up at a place called Thornbrake Hill by men but The Tomb of Dancing Myrina by the gods. The Dardanians were led by Aphrodite's son Aeneas, men from Zeleia in the foothills of Mount Ida by the archer Pandarus. Others were from Adresteia and the land of Apaesus led by the doomed sons of Merops. Men from Percote, Practius, Sestus, Abydos and Arisbe were led by Asius.

Hippothöus commanded the Pelasgian spearmen; Acamas and Peiros led Thracians; Euphemus led the Cicones. Paeonians with curved bows were led by Pyraechmes. Hairy Pylaemenes led the Paphlagonians, Odius and Epistrophus the Alizones, Chromis and Ennomus the Mysians. Phorcys and godlike Ascanius led the Phrygians, Nastes and Amphimacus the Carians.

Last and greatest of all was Sarpedon and the faultless Glaucus leading Lycians from the far-off wild waters of the river Xanthus.

Book 3

Now the Trojans advanced, screaming like wildfowl, clamouring like cranes flying south in the winter, while the Greeks by contrast marched fast and silently to meet them, the dust of the plain billowing up a like a mountain mist about their feet, so thick that it closed visibility down to just a few yards.

As the armies met, Paris leapt from the ranks of the Trojans, armed with his bow and sword and brandishing a brace of javelins, over his shoulders a great leopard's skin, screaming a challenge to any Greek to meet him man to man. Menelaus heard, saw him and happy as a famished lion spotting a carrion carcase or fat deer, leapt down from his chariot and ran forward. Seeing him, Paris promptly melted back into the ranks of his men.

Then his brother Hector rounded on him. "Paris, you empty-headed gigolo, you should have died long ago or never been born at all rather than live to bring such pain and disgrace on us all. You were braver than this when you sailed from home to steal the wife of a man with powerful friends and kin, a grief to your father and city and to yourself nothing but a shame. Now you haven't even courage to face Menelaus, knowing well that pretty-boy looks and a nice hair-do win few battles. Still, we Trojans are to blame as well as you, for if we were not just as weak-headed, we would long since have stoned you out of our gates for the grief you have caused us."

"Hector, I can neither answer nor argue away what you say," his brother admitted miserably. "Unlike you, I am not a man of inexhaustible energy and strength, with a heart like a workman's axe that relentlessly shapes the toughest ship's timbers – but you should not despise gifts that may be softer but are also god-given, gifts no man could win just by hankering after them. Still, if you think this quarrel is best settled by me and Menelaus alone, then tell the Greeks and Trojans to lay down their weapons while he and I fight for Helen and all her possessions. Then afterwards everyone will be able to swear oaths of peace and live in friendship again."

So Hector strode happily and boldly into the space between the battalions, forcing them apart. Seeing him, Agamemnon shouted to his fellow-Greeks to hold off — at which all on both sides fell silent.

"You Greeks and Trojans," Hector roared, "Paris asks that you lay down your arms while he and Menelaus fight alone for Helen and all her possessions."

Menelaus answered him. "As the injured party in this quarrel, I accept his challenge so that when one of us is dead, the living rest can be friends again. Now let two lambs, one of them black, one white, for the earth and the sun, be brought here and sacrificed as pledges of peace. Only let old Priam make the pledges. I do not trust his sons."

Happy at the prospect of the war's end, Greeks and Trojans now both laid aside their weapons and armour while Hector sent heralds to fetch the animals for sacrifice and bring Priam with them. Now, too, the gods' messenger Iris in the guise of her sister-in-law Laodice went to white-armed Helen in her room where she sat weaving a large tapestry.

"Quick, sweetie!" the goddess urged, "come and see what is happening! The armies have put down their weapons and Menelaus and Paris will fight for you! You are to be their prize!"

Her news filled Helen's heart with love and longing for her first husband, parents and old home. Weeping, she threw on her shining cape and with two handmaidens ran to the city wall by the Scaean Gate. There Priam stood with Trojan elders now too frail to fight but all still men, for as Helen approached they fell silent, murmuring softly to each other: "Who could blame Trojans and Greeks for fighting over such a woman? Still, lovely as she is, let her leave and sail away rather than stay to be a grief to us and our children."

"Come, sit beside me, child," Priam called to her, "and tell me about these people since you know them well. Who is that imposing man over there – a head taller than anyone else around him?"

"That is Atreus' son Agamemnon," Helen answered. "He was my brother-in-law once, slut that I am, back in a time that now seems a dream."

"Fortunate Agamemnon," the other murmured. "I fought a war in Phrygia once but never saw anything like the number of Greeks I see here now. Who is that other near him, shorter by a head but huge across the chest and shoulders, like some mighty bellwether?"

"That is Laertes' son, quick-witted Odysseus. He rules in poor and rocky Ithaca."

Antenor endorsed what she said. "Odysseus and Menelaus both stayed with me once, a long time ago," he recalled. "Menelaus was the more imposing while they were on their feet, but Odysseus much the more so when they sat down. Menelaus spoke little and that little simply and clearly.

Odysseus you would have thought an idiot – until he opened his mouth. Then he became the most impressive speaker you can imagine."

"And that huge man with them?" asked Priam.

"Ajax, tower of the Greeks," answered Helen. "Beyond him stands Idomeneus and other Cretan captains. I know most of those I can see – but do not see my own brothers Castor and Polydeuces. Probably they were too ashamed of me to come to theTroad.'[9] She was not to know, of course, that in fact they were already dead and long since buried.

Now, from out of the city, heralds took sacrificial lambs together with wine and cups of gold. Idaeus carried these and informed Priam of their purpose.

"Sir, you are called by the chief men on both sides to seal truce pledges."

So the old man's chariot was made ready and he rode to the assembly where Agamemnon and Odysseus awaited him. Heralds then prepared the sacrifice and poured water over the chiefs' hands.

"Father Zeus," Agamemnon prayed in a loud voice, "and all you powers of under-earth, take vengeance on anyone who breaks this oath, which is that if Paris kills Menelaus, he may keep Helen and all her possessions, while if Menelaus kills Paris, then the Trojans will restore Helen and all her possessions and pay due compensation to the Greeks."

Then he cut the lambs' throats and drew wine from bowls into cups, after which everyone present, Greek and Trojan, swore to the oath as well. "May great Zeus and all other

---

[9]

The ancient region of what is now Turkey, whose chief city was Troy.

immortals spill the brains of any man who breaks this oath," they called, "as we now spill this wine."

But none of all this would Zeus fulfill. Unable to watch the fight, Priam laid the dead lambs in the chariot, whipped up his horses and returned quickly to Troy while Hector and Odysseus measured out the arena and shook lots in a brazen helmet to decide who should have first spear-cast. As they did so, all on both sides prayed silently and devoutly to Zeus that whichever of the fighters was truly responsible for the war would now pay with his life so that the rest of them could settle down in peace and friendship.

Paris's lot fell out first, so he and Menelaus quickly armed themselves in greaves,[10] corslet, sword, shield, plumed helmet and a huge spear each. Then, raging, roaring, shaking their spears, each took up position. Paris threw first. His spear crashed full into the middle of Menelaus' shield but failed to penetrate it, the point bending back. Then Menelaus prayed and threw. His spear hit Paris' shield flush in the centre and crashed on through but still failed to hit the man behind. So now he went for him with his sword – which shivered on impact with the crest of Paris's helmet. Swearing and groaning in frustration, the Greek chief grabbed his enemy by the helmet and seemed likely to strangle him as he dragged him back towards his army's lines, but Aphrodite rescued her favourite by snapping the chinstrap, then wrapping him in a mist in which she carried him back to his own perfumed bedroom in Troy. There, disguising herself as the old woman

---

[10]

The metal shin-guard fastening behind the calf.

who was her favourite wool-worker, she hurried to find Helen.

"Come home quickly," she cackled. "Paris is in his room on his great bed and can't wait to get his hands on you. He looks so handsome, you would never guess he had just been fighting a duel."

Helen was troubled, recognizing Aphrodite in spite of her disguise. "Strange goddess, why do you keep me in your power? Is it because Menelaus has beaten Paris and you cannot bear to see me taken back to Greece? Or do you plan to carry me even further from here, to be the plaything of some other favourite of yours? If you like Paris so much, why don't give up your godhead and become his wife or sex slave yourself? I have had enough of him and refuse to pleasure him ever again. Besides, the Trojan women would despise me if I took him back now – and I have more than enough to put up with from them already."

Aphrodite flashed at her angrily in reply. "Be careful, girl, that I do not end by hating you as much as I now love you – perhaps even abandon you for the Trojans and Greeks to fight over your dead body."

So frightened Helen did as she was told but spoke bitterly to Paris when she joined him. "What a pity you came home again" she railed. "You claimed you were a better man than Menelaus. Why don't you challenge him again to prove it?"

"Lady, with the gods' help he beat me this time," Paris answered her simply. "Another time, I will beat him. But come to bed now. Never since I first saw you have I wanted you so much as I do now."

So the lovers went to bed while Menelaus still raged and ranged up and down the lines of Greeks and Trojans searching for his prey.

Book 4

Sitting in council, a gold cup in his hand, Zeus made fun of his wife Hera and daughter, contrasting what seemed their indifference to the fate of their favourites fighting in the war with the care Aphrodite had just shown Paris. He suggested they arrange a peaceful outcome to events so that Troy might after all survive while Menelaus returned home with Helen. Hera, though, accused him of deliberately thwarting their wishes, so the father of gods agreed she might provoke hostilities again – so long as Trojans broke the truce-oaths first and so were responsible for what happened to them.

So Athene flashed down to earth and prompted Pandarus to take a bow-shot at Menelaus, which he did, getting his men to shield him while he strung the weapon and loosed an arrow, hitting the Greek chief on the stout buckle joining the halves of his corslet and penetrating beyond - though not deeply enough to do him serious injury. Immediately, seeing the arrow in his side and the blood flooding down his brother's legs, Agamemnon panicked, blamed the Trojans for the truce-breaking and threatened destruction of their city in revenge. Menelaus though, calmed him while Machaon, son of the great healer Asclepius, dressed the wound and applied healing and anaesthetic drugs.

Still the war restarted, with Agamemnon now going about the army lifting morale. He visited Idomeneus and his Cretans, then the two Ajaxes and old Nestor of Pylos – even accused Menestheus and Odysseus of hanging back. He reproached Diomedes, recalling a time when the other's father Tydeus, ambushed by fifty Cadmeians, killed them all except for a single ambusher in obedience to Zeus' command.[11]

Now too Ares fired up the Trojans with fear and hatred, they being so multi-tongued that few of them could understand all the others. First Antilochus killed the Trojan Echepolus, while Agenor killed Elephenor as the other tried to seize the body and strip it of its armour. Then Telamonian Ajax killed Anthemion who fell like a graceful black poplar cut by some wheelwright to fashion wheels from, while Antiphus, Priam's son, killed Leucus, a companion of Odysseus, with a spear-throw. In revenge, Odysseus struck down Democoön, one of Priam's bastard sons.

So the slaughter continued, Apollo roaring on the Trojans while Athene did the same for the Greeks. Trojan Peirus killed Diores by smashing his leg with a stone, then spearing him as he tried to hobble away in agony. Aetolian Thoas revenged the dead man, though, by spearing Peirus in the chest as he ran back to his lines, then finished him off with the sword. So the fighting thundered on with only the dead on both sides silent and motionless. Indeed many men ended that day sprawled face-down in the dust.

----

[11]

An early example of the way Homer draws in epic material from other sources. Diomedes' father Tydeus was one of the famous 'Seven Against Thebes' in the wars that followed the death of Oedipus.

Book 5

Next it was the turn of Diomedes, son of Tydeus, to do great things.[12] Attacked by the two sons of Dares, priest of Hephaestus, he first killed Phegeus with a spear in the chest. Then, even although the god rescued the man's brother Idaeus to be a lone comfort for their bereaved old father, he seized their chariot and horses as spoils.

Next, after Athene and Ares had left the fighting for fear of Zeus' anger, Agamemnon killed Odius, chief of the Halizones, while Idomeneus killed Phaestus and Menelaus killed the hunter Scamandrius. Meriones then killed Phereclus – the craftsman who first built Paris' deadly ships[13] – while Meges killed Pedaeus, a son of Trojan Antenor, with a spear thrust through the back of the neck as he ran away from him. The man died biting the cold bronze. Meanwhile Eurypylus used his sword to lop off Lypsenor's life along with one of his arms.

So the fighters went about their work while Diomedes raged still further ahead - until Pandarus hit him with another

---

[12]

Throughout the epic, heroes (mainly Greek) are singled out so that Homer can demonstrate at length their courage, and prowess. Diomedes here is the first.

[13]

In which he sailed to visit Menelaus and stole his wife.

arrow, this one in the shoulder and crowed that now he was a dead man. Hearing him, though, Diomedes got Sthenelus his charioteer to push the arrow clean through the wound, praying to Athene who calmed his pain while encouraging him to fight on against all he met except gods — although even so, she added, he might attack Aphrodite if that goddess crossed his path.

So Diomedes returned to the fighting, killing Astynous and Hypeirion, then Polyeidus and Abas, sons of the dream-interpreter Eurydamas. Then he killed the twin sons of Phaenops, Xanthus and Thoön, then Echemmon and Chromius, two more of Priam's sons.

Seeing him apparently unstoppable, Aeneas looked about for Pandarus to ask why his bow was not being worked, but Pandarus answered that he was disheartened, having already shot at two great Greeks including Diomedes that day but killed neither. Perhaps, he grumbled, he should have left his bow at home and brought his chariot instead. So Aeneas invited him either to manage his team while he himself fought with the spear — or fight while he himself did the driving. Thinking Aeneas' horses would be more responsive to their master's touch on the reins, Pandarus chose the spear-work, so these two made straight for Diomedes. Coming close, Pandarus smashed his spear straight through the other's shield and corslet — but the other, who had avoided the point, killed him with a return throw in the face, between nose and eye, so now Aeneas had to jump down to guard the body and prevent it from being stripped —only to be felled in his turn by a rock thrown by Diomedes which smashed his hip. His goddess mother Aphrodite had to save him then while Diomedes' troops seized his chariot with its fabled horses bred of stock presented by great Zeus himself to Trojan Laomedon.

Meanwhile and as they did so, Diomedes chased after Aphrodite and wounded her with a spear-thrust through the hand - at which she gave a great shriek and dropped her wounded son Aeneas.

"Stick to your sultry love potions, goddess," Diomedes shouted after her. "Leave the fighting to men."

So Phoebus Apollo had to protect Aeneas instead while Aphrodite borrowed her brother Ares' chariot to fly weeping to her mother. There on Olympus, Dione comforted her, soothed her pain - and reminded her that no good ever came to mortal men who fought against gods.[14] Hera and Athene, though, teased her and Zeus mercilessly.

Meanwhile, back on earth, still raging to finish off Aeneas, Diomedes had to be beaten off three times by Phoebus Apollo himself before the god could carry the wounded man to his own temple at Pergamon[15] where Leto and Artemis healed him, leaving a phantom double of the Trojan chieftain on the battlefield to be fought over by both sides. The archer-god also recruited Ares to stop the impetuous Diomedes, so the murderous war god went among the Trojans disguised as the Thracian chief Acamas, urging them to come to Aeneas's rescue.

Meanwhile Sarpedon turned on Hector. "How is it that I, an ally of yours with no personal stake in Troy, am doing all I

---

[14]

According to later legend which Virgil used later in the *Aeneid*, Aphrodite got her revenge by making Diomedes' wife unfaithful and forcing him to wander away to Italy after the fall of Troy.

[15]

The citadel of Troy. Later a city in NW Asia Minor where parchment originated from.

can to help," he asked, "while you Trojans lose heart and turn away where there is work to be done?"

Shamed by the reproach, Hector stormed out of his chariot, shook his spears and encouraged his men to turn and attack. Now, too, Apollo restored the healed Aeneas to the Trojans so that, aided by the god Ares, they finally halted the Greeks' advance. But then the two Ajaxes, Odysseus, Diomedes and Menelaus rallied the Greeks in turn. Menelaus killed Deicoön, one of Aeneas' companions, with a spear thrust in the belly, while Aeneas killed Orsilochus and Crethon, sons of Diocles. But then Menelaus and Antilochus, old Nestor's son, confronted Aeneas, thwarting him from stripping his victims of their armour.

Meanwhile Menelaus killed Pylaemenes, chief of the Paphlagonians, and Antilochus killed Mydon, his charioteer, with a sword-thrust through the side of the head. But now Hector and the war-god charged in from their side, killing Menesthes and Anchialus in the same chariot. Intent on revenge, Telamonian Ajax then killed Amphius — but could not strip him of his armour either, being beaten back by the Trojans. Next, Sarpedon and Tlepolemus threw at the same instant — Tlepolemus being killed outright by a hit in the throat while Sarpedon, struck in the thigh, had to be carried out of the fighting with the other's spear still dangling out of him. Odysseus considered swooping in to finish off the great Lycian but directed his anger at his companions instead, not being fated to kill Zeus's own son.[16] So he killed Coeranus,

---

[16] Do we choose all our actions freely or are we at the mercy of our genes, social conditioning and so on? Homer sensibly sees both as shaping out will.

Alastor, Chromios, Alcander, Halius, Noemon and Prytanis instead before Hector could storm up to relieve his assault, killing in his turn Teuthras, Orestes, Trechus, Oenomaus and Oresbius the Boeotian. Meanwhile under an oak tree as all this went on, Pelagon, a companion of Sarpedon, pushed Tlepolemus' spear through the chief's thigh to free it. His patient fainted with the pain.

Seeing Ares on the rampage in company with Hector of the Trojans, Hera and Athene thought to re-enter the fighting and stop him, so while Hebe harnessed their chariot, Athene armed, grabbed her spear and complained about Ares' interference to the god of gods who sat brooding alone on the highest point of Mount Olympus. So Zeus listened and gave permission for what they intended, whereupon the two goddesses swooped down to where the Simoïs and Scamander rivers join, hobbling their horses there and drifting a protective mist about them.

While Hera took on the likeness of bronze-voiced Stentor,[17] whose voice could drown out fifty ordinary fighters, urging the Greeks on to even greater efforts, Athene made for Diomedes' chariot where she found the hero bathing his arrow-wound - now made doubly agonising because of the salt in his sweat. She reproached him for leaving the action, but he reminded her that she herself had told him not to stand

---

As here, men act of their own accord for their own reasons - while also doing what fate and the gods intend.

[17]

Such has been Homer's influence on later literature and language that Stentor's loud voice still gives us 'stentorian', just as Hector's style in English stage performance gave us 'hectoring'.

against gods, Aphrodite alone, excepted, so now Athene gave him permission to attack even Ares — turning Sthenelus, his driver, out of the chariot so as to take his place with the reins.

"Don't be afraid of the war-god who is a maniac and fights for the Trojans," she shouted. "I will help you."

So Diomedes and the goddess bore down on mighty Ares who, seeing them approach as he stripped the armour from Periphas' corpse, grabbed his spear and thrust murderously at Diomedes over the horses' reins. Athene, though, caught the shaft and deflected it while leaning on Diomedes' spear arm to drive it full and low down into the war-god's belly. Then Greeks and Trojans alike stopped fighting in stark terror at the appalling scream that arose, as of nine or ten thousand ordinary injured men, from the wounded war god's throat who there and then lost all appetite for battle and fled skyward like the cloud column of a mighty storm.

Limping raging and tearful to father Zeus on Mount Olympus, he showed his blood and pain, blaming the goddesses Hera and Athene for encouraging Diomedes. Zeus, though, refused to sympathise, telling his awesome brat instead to stop whining. But for the fact that he was his son, he said, he would himself long since have been thrown him out of the company of other gods. Still, there it was: his own son *was* an immortal, so he gave orders for Paean to heal him, and soon, treated, bathed and dressed, the other once again took his place at the Olympian feasting, strong and violent as ever.

Book 6

Meanwhile down on the plain of Troy, battle raged on. Telemonian Ajax killed huge Acamus while Diomedes sent the hospitable Axylus down to death's realm together with his charioteer Calesius. Euryalus killed Dresus and Opheltius, then Aesopus and Pedasus, stripping them of their armour, while Polypoetes cut down Astyalus. Pidytes fell to Odysseus, noble Aretaon to Teucer, Ablerus to Nestor's son Antilochus, Elatus to great Agamemnon. Laitus killed Phylacus, while Melanthius fell to Eurypylus.

Amid all this carnage, Menelaus of the tremendous war cry captured Adrestus whose chariot was smashed when his horses bolted. He was thinking of sparing the man's life in return for a hefty ransom, but just then his brother Agamemnon ran up to remind him of how the Trojans had insulted him, whereupon he shoved Adrestus away for Agamemnon himself to finish off. Nestor then urged the rest of the Greeks to show no mercy either. There would be time for plunder, he told them, when all the Trojans were dead.

Now Priam's son, the seer Helenus, advised his brother Hector to return to the city to tell the women to offer prayers and sacrifice to Athene while Aeneas and other Trojan heroes held the Greeks at bay. So Hector did as the other suggested, but and as they talked, Glaucus jumped into the space between the armies to confront Diomedes – who saw and challenged him.

"Who are you, stranger?" Diomedes shouted. "I will fight you if you are a Trojan, but not if you are a god, for everyone knows that those who fight with gods do not live long, as Lycurgus famously found out when he so terrified the god Dionysus that Zeus struck him blind."

"The generations of men are like leaves that fall uncounted and uncountable, yet are restored every year," Glaucus shouted back. "If you must know me, there was once a famous man called Sisyphus whose grandson was the handsome Bellerophon. Proetus's wife Anteia lusted after him, but he refused her invitation to sex, so she complained to her husband that he had tried to rape her. Proetus dared not have the man put to death, so he sent him instead to the king of Lycia with sinister symbols[18] indicating that he was to be killed. So the Lycian king ordered him to kill the monster Chimaera,[19] which he did, and after that he fought against the Solymi and the Amazons. On his return, the king laid an ambush for him, but when Bellerephon killed even those lying in wait, the other realized he must be born a god and so begged him to stay and gave him his daughter in marriage instead together with half his kingdom while the other Lycians presented him with magnificent vineyards and cornfields."

"Three children were born to Bellerophon: Isander, Hippolochus and a daughter called Laodameia who slept with

---

[18]

He may mean letters - in which case Homer is describing the first known written death warrant!

[19]

A mythical monster with a lion's head, goat's body and dragon's tail, later put to use in Virgil's Underworld to punish sinners.

Zeus and bore great Sarpedon. I am son to Hippolochus, and my grandfather Bellerophon taught me always to strive to be best so as not to disgrace my fathers and others of my line."

Diomedes planted his spear in the earth. "Then we are linked by ties of friendship," he declared, "for my grandfather Oeneus entertained Bellerophon twenty days in his house. He gave him a purple war-belt and received in return a gold two-handled cup. You and I are friends, so let us avoid each other in battle and exchange armour instead. There are plenty of other enemies for us both to kill."

Then they both jumped down from their chariots and exchanged armour — only Zeus must have stolen Glaucus's wits, because he exchanged gold armour for Diomedes' bronze gear, a hundred oxen's worth for the value of nine.

Meanwhile Hector came to the Scaean gate where he was immediately surrounded by Trojan wives, daughters and mothers all begging for news of their men. Eventually he came to Priam's great palace whose main building boasted fifty apartments in which the king's sons slept with their wives, his daughters in twelve other rooms with his sons-in-law, their husbands. Here Hector was met by his mother and sister.

"Why have you left the battle, darling son?' asked his mother. "Have you come to pray? Let me bring wine for you to pour to father Zeus and refresh yourself."

"Mother," answered Hector, "covered with blood as I am, I am in no state to sacrifice to great Zeus — or to get drunk. No, I want you and all the other women to sacrifice and pray to Athene while I try to persuade my brother Paris back to the fighting, although I wish he were dead for all the harm he has caused us."

So his mother did as he asked while he went over to Paris's house and found his brother polishing his weapons and armour. Under the reproach of both Hector and Helen, the other agreed to return to the fighting, claiming only to have been depressed — but now cheered by hope of better fortune. And so he arranged to follow Hector who himself returned to his own house where a maid told him that his wife and small son had gone to the great tower of Troy to view the battle which, rumour claimed, the Greeks were winning. So Hector returned to the Scaean gate to be there met by his wife with the baby he called Scamandrius but everyone else called Astyanax.

"Hector," his wife wailed, "you are all I have left since Achilles killed my father Eëtion and my seven brothers in Cilician Thebe. For my sake, do not take so many risks. Defend us in greater safety here, by our tower."

"Lady," her husband answered, "it is my duty always to fight in front of my men. Deep in my heart I know Troy will one day die, but I could not face the shame were I to hide like coward — or live to see you carried off as a prize by victorious Greeks."

Then he stretched out his hands to take his infant son who screamed at the sight of the huge helmet with its nodding plumes. Laughing, he took it off to play with him. "Great Zeus," he prayed, "may my son grow up brave and strong so that one day men may say he was better than his father."

Then he handed his son to his wife again who smiled back at him through her tears. Moved, he stroked her hand. "Andromache," he urged, "try not to be unhappy. Nobody goes down to death one moment sooner or later than fate decrees, so now go back to your work, as I must to mine."

Hector then returned to the war while his wife went back to their house where the women lamented as though he were already dead. Paris caught up with him as he left the city.

"Brother," he said, "I am sorry if I hung back."

"Brother," answered Hector, "no man could ever fault either your fighting or your courage, and I am tired of hearing you reviled by the Trojans whose plight you brought on them. If I myself have been too hard on you, I will make up for it, if Zeus ever allows us to drive these Greeks from Troy."[20]

---

[20]

These "scenes" of Hector with his wife, son and brother are among the noblest and most touching in the *Iliad* - yet given to Trojan rather than a Greek. A few lines earlier, Hector knew Troy was doomed - but seems to have forgotten by the end.

Book 7

To the relief of the tiring Trojans, Hector and Paris now swept into the battle. Straight away Paris killed Menesthius of Arne while Hector speared Eioneus in the neck. Then Glaucus, casting across a crowd of men, downed Iphinous with a spear in the shoulder as the man was climbing into his chariot. Seeing the slaughter, Athene flashed down from Olympus — but was intercepted by Apollo.

"Why have you come to help the Greeks win?" he asked. "One day, I know, Troy is doomed to fall since you goddesses hate it so much, but for the time being it would be better to stop the fighting."

"Very well," the goddess answered. "But how?"

"Let us inspire Hector to issue a man-to-man challenge so that the others will lay down their weapons to watch."

Then the seer Helenus, Priam's son, divining the god's intentions, broached the same idea to his brother. "Hector," he said, "make the Trojans and Greeks sit down by issuing a man-to-man challenge. You can do it in safety since I know it is not your fate to die today."

Falling in with the idea, Hector parted the armies and shouted his challenge, adding as a condition that the loser might be stripped of armour but his body be given back for burial.

Wary and confused, the Greeks were silent until Menelaus, ashamed, jumped up to accept. Luckily for him, though, his brother Agamemnon restrained him while ancient Nestor harangued the other Greeks, demanding another volunteer, recalling a time when the men of his own city, Pylos, were challenged in the same way by their enemies' best man, Ereuthalion, who wore marvellous armour won originally by mighty Lycurgus from the mace-wielding Areïthous. He himself, he said, had taken up that challenge — and won it.

Spurred to bravery by his story,[21] Agamemnon himself, Diomedes, the Ajaxes, Idomeneus the Cretan and Meriones, Eurypylus, Thoas and Odysseus then all got up. So Nestor cast lots in a helmet and out jumped that of Telamonian Ajax — which pleased everyone. That great fighter then quickly armed himself again, seized his spear, stalked forward and squared up to Hector.

The Trojan threw first, and his spear pierced six of the layers of Ajax's shield but stopped at the and final one. Then the other threw, piercing Hector's shield but missing the man behind, who swerved. Each then pulled his weapon free and threw again from closer range. This time Ajax's boss deflected Hector's point while his own spear again tore through, this time drawing blood. Now both men drew their swords and rushed at each other, but the outcome after long fighting being inconclusive, the heralds on both sides, Talthybius and Idaeus, stepped between and parted them with their staves, proposing an honourable truce since night was fast falling.

"Put it to Hector," answered Ajax to Trojan Idaeus, "for he proposed the duel."

---

[21]

Nestor is not just a garrulous old man. His stories of old heroes are meant to encourage and inspire bravery in his hearers - as are the *Iliad* itself and all such tales of the bards.

"Ajax," answered the other, "you are a great fighter, and we can always meet again. For now, let us part honourably, as friends."

So Hector gave Ajax his silver-studded sword while the other gave him a brilliant purple war-belt, and both men were then helped back to their lines by friends. Afterwards the Greeks feasted and Nestor proposed a truce for the next day so that both sides could burn their dead and the Greeks build a wall to protect their beached ships against the chance that one day the Trojans might press them back. This proposal was agreed while the Trojans and their allies also feasted and debated. Pointing out that they were in the wrong for having broken the earlier truce, Antenor advised handing Helen and all her property back to the Greeks. Paris, though, bluntly and angrily refused, adding that he would be willing to return Helen's property together with more of his own as well by way of compensation.

Then Priam pronounced judgement. "Trojans and allies," he said, "let Idaeus put Paris's proposal to the Greeks tomorrow. At that time they can arrange a truce so that both sides may bury their dead."

And so it came about. Next dawning, Idaeus went down to the Greek ships to convey Paris's offer. Diomedes advised against acceptance since he thought the Trojans were losing anyway, and the rest agreed with him while accepting the Trojans' other proposal, and so all day both sides gathered wood, built pyres and cremated their dead. The Greeks also started work on a wall to protect their ships, fashioning a rampart and ditch with sharpened stakes and constructing a pair of great doors to let men and chariots through.

The gods themselves looked on in astonishment at this bold effort, and Poseidon grew angry. "Zeus," he complained, "how dare these mortals build a wall that will one day be more famous even than the one Apollo and I built for Laomedon[22] without making sacrifice to us first?"

Zeus pacified the Earth-shaker. "Brother," he declared, "let lesser gods worry about such lesser matters. After the Greeks have sailed home, there will be nothing to stop you demolishing their wall."

On the night of the second day following all this, though, while the men on both sides feasted and slept, Zeus thundered ominously.

---

[22] In an earlier generation, Poseidon and Apollo built a city wall for the then Trojan king Laomedon who afterwards refused to pay them.

Book 8

As dawn covered the sky like a gold cloak again, Zeus called the gods to a conference. "I have decided," he said, "to make an end of this business, so let no-one presume to contradict what I say or lend any help to either side from now on, for if they do, I will whip them back to Olympus. Or down to Tartarus. Or even tie them up and leave them dangling in the space between."

Having spoken so menacingly, he harnessed his bronze-shod horses to his chariot and sped down to Mount Ida[23] where he crouched and looked out over the city of Troy and the Greek ships. By that time battle had restarted. The young fighters on both sides had armed, collided, and the air was full of shouts, screams and the thunder of bronze on bronze. As when at midday the sun-god balances his scales in mid-heaven, so now the father of gods balanced his scales – and the Greeks' death day showed the heavier.[24]

---

[23]

A mountain on the southern boundary of Troy's plain (called the Troad) but also a mountain in Crete where, it was thought, Zeus himself was born in a cave.

[24]

Again, Homer is ambiguous. Men determine their own fates, yet the gods can and do interfere to shape them for their own ends - while great events at least are known in advance and fixed by destiny anyway.

Now the Trojans proved the stronger, so that none of the great Greeks, not Idomeneus, Agamemnon nor the two Ajaxes, could hold his ground against them. Only Nestor actually failed to retreat in good time, and that was only because one of Paris's arrows had mortally wounded the third horse in his chariot team. Now, as a result, Hector closed in so fast that the old man was likely to be killed — but Diomedes, having failed to stop Odysseus's retreat with the others, turned back alone to the old man's rescue. Leaving their charioteers to handle the old man's stricken team, he took the other into his own chariot and even killed Hector's charioteer with a spear-cast. Zeus thundered a warning for him to retreat with the others, though, unwilling as he was to leave Hector to boast that he had run away.

Hearing Zeus's thunder, Hector urged his men the harder, encouraging them to jump the Greeks' new ditch and wall and fire their ships, or at least send them scurrying aboard to sail for home. Hearing his high words, Hera was angry and badgered Poseidon, without success, to intervene, while Hector roared on, but at least the goddess stiffened Agamemnon's backbone, encouraging him to make a stand by Odysseus's ships in the centre. There the great chief was just then praying for a deliverance that great Zeus assured him of by way of an omen in the form of a marauding eagle overhead that just then dropped its prey, a young faun, right beside his altar.

So now the chief men of the Greeks turned and fought outside their ditch and wall. Teucer[25] the archer dropped

---

[25] A cousin of Hector but also half-brother of the Greek Telemonian Ajax.

Trojan after Trojan with his arrows, always scampering back afterwards to the protection of Telamonian Ajax's shield. Time after time he aimed at Hector but hit others instead, including Gorgythion, another of Priam's sons, whose head drooped and fell on his shoulders like a poppy bowed by Spring rains when he was hit.[26] Screaming with rage, Hector now made for the archer, caught up a jagged rock and smashed his arm and shoulder with it.

His half-brother protected him, but filled now with Zeus's fury, all the Trojans attacked so hard that the Greeks were forced back over their ditch and sharpened stakes. Hera tried to persuade Athene to interfere, whereupon Zeus's daughter armed, seized her spear and mounted her chariot – but the chief of gods saw her and sent golden-winged Iris to warn that she would spend ten long years recovering from his lightning strike if she defied him, so she returned to Olympus instead, followed by Zeus himself who once more warned his fellow Olympians against trying to stem the Trojan advance until Patroclus had been killed and Achilles restored to the fighting.

Meanwhile, Hector once more called an assembly of the Trojans and their allies at which he proposed that they camp on the plain nearby and resume their attempt on the ships next day, first, though, sending to Troy for provisions and ordering the city's youths and old men to mount guard along its walls. All this was done as he suggested, with the result that later, by starlight, a thousand watch-fires of the Greeks and Trojans

---

26

One of Homer's often unexpectedly beautiful short similes (rhetorical comparisons).

gleamed and flared, the sentries standing beside them with their fodder-chomping horses.

Book 9

Now it was the Greeks' turn to suffer despair and fear. At an assembly summoned by him, their weeping commander-in-chief proposed that they abandon the expedition and go home. For a while all were silent. Then, though, Diomedes burst out.

"Agamemnon, since we are in assembly, you will forgive me if I speak my mind and say you are a coward or a fool or both. If running away suits you, very well then, run — but the rest of us will stay and fight. Or if they all want to run too, then Sthelenus and I will stay here alone to sack Troy since that is what we came here to do."

When the others shouted their agreement, Nestor stood up quickly. "Son of Tydeus, you are among the best of your generation for brains as well as bravery, but now is not a good time to be arguing. Let us shelve business for the day, eat our dinners in peace and post guards since the enemy is close by."

His advice being accepted by the assembly, seven of the best young commanders, each with a company of a hundred men, were posted between the armies as a barrier and early alarm. Meanwhile, once more at Nestor's suggestion, Agamemnon feasted all his senior commanders.

"Agamemnon, greatest of men," the old man firmly resumed, "now I must tell you what *I* think. For your sake and ours, you must placate Achilles whom you injured and offended. You must do whatever is needed to bring him back into the fighting.'

Agamemnon agreed instantly. "I was mad to quarrel with that great fighter whom Zeus loves so much and I now want to pay for my mistake. I will offer him seven perfect tripods,[27] ten talents[28] of gold, twenty cauldrons and ten race-proven horses. I will also offer him seven women from Lesbos as well as the girl Briseis whom I took from him – and whom I will swear a great oath that I never touched. All these will be his, but besides them, if the gods grant that we ever sack the city, he may fill his ship with Trojan gold and bronze and have first choice of twenty Trojan women. Finally, if it is given to both of us to return home safely to Argos, he may pick whichever of my daughters he wants to marry and thereby become my son-in-law. He need pay no bride-price, and I will dower her with seven fortified settlements."

"Great Agamemnon," answered Nestor, "it would be hard for anyone to despise or reject such gifts, so let Phoenix, Telamonian Ajax and Odysseus go with the heralds Odius and Eurybates to convey this offer to Achilles."

After due ceremony then, all these walked along the beach to Achilles' camp where they found him playing his lyre and singing heroic stories. Patroclus was with him. Noting the visitors' approach, he broke off and jumped up.

---

[27]

A three-legged iron cauldron and standard Homeric gift - virtually a kind of currency.

[28]

An ancient unit of weight, probably around 35 kilos.

"Welcome, best of all my friends," he greeted them. "Patroclus, give our visitors a drink."

Patroclus did so and afterwards spitted the backs of a sheep and a goat and the chine of a whole hog while Automedon made up the fire, spread the meats out over the hot coals and salted them. When all was ready, they feasted, and afterwards Ajax prompted Phoenix with a nod — but Odysseus, lifting his wine cup, spoke instead.

"Here's to your health, Achilles. You have given us all the entertainment men could want, but I have to tell you we feel more fear than happiness, for soon our ships are likely to be lost to the rampaging Trojans. Zeus is on their side and no-one can stand up to marauding Hector. Only you can save us, and if you refuse, I do not see how you will be able to forgive yourself. Your own father warned you when you left home always to control your temper, while if the injury Agamemnon did you still rankles, then listen to the magnificent compensation he offers." He reeled off the list of everything Agamemnon had promised,[29] but Achilles' answer was blunt.

"Odysseus, I plainly tell you that I think Agamemnon will never persuade me. After we came to Troy, I did more than my share of the fighting and made over to him all the prizes I won – and for what? We came here to avenge a stolen woman, yet he stole mine. Are the sons of Atreus alone in

---

[29]

In the Greek, Odysseus repeats Agamemnon's offer word for word - usual Homeric practice along with stock phrases and descriptions that made it easier for the old-time bards to remember the immense amount of material they had to recite.

loving their women? No, he and you will have to work out some other way of saving the ships and your skins. In fact tomorrow, if you care to watch, you may see me and my men embark for home. Why should I stay and fight for wealth and women? I can get all I need of those at home, while a life once lost is lost for ever. My mother Thetis told me long ago that I could either fight here and die young – but win undying glory – or live a long, happy and inglorious life at home. I now choose that other fate. Tell Agamemnon so. Phoenix can stay if he wants, though, and sail with me tomorrow."

At that, Phoenix burst into tears. "My child, how could I stay here without you? Long ago my father took a mistress, and in her bitterness, my mother persuaded me to bed the girl myself so as to turn her against him. I did so, and in revenge my father persuaded the Furies to prevent me from ever having children of my own. I almost killed him for it but eventually made my way to your father's palace instead where ever since you have been like a son to me. Please, Achilles, learn to control your anger. Remember, there are spirits of prayer that are lame and slow – and a spirit of ruin that is strong and fast. When ruin leads men astray, prayers follow as healers, but if you turn your back on them, they appeal to Zeus for punishment. No man could blame you before Agamemnon made his offer. Now, though, you should give way. Great men have always let themselves be persuaded by great gifts. In olden days, Curetes[30] and Aetolians fought over

---

[30] Mythical athletes and dancers associated with Cretan Zeus.

the city of Calydon, and trouble flared when Meleager[31] with other heroes killed a huge boar sent by Artemis to ravage the land, after which they all fell out over sharing out the beast's grisly head and hide. For as long as Meleager fought for the city, the Curetes were beaten back, but when he got angry with his mother and stayed at home, they almost managed to sack it. Only with gifts was he persuaded at the last moment to fight again, and so the city was saved, even though he never did get the gifts he was promised."

Achilles' response was short and harsh. "Phoenix, my revered old friend and tutor, stop trying to tug at my heart-strings and taking Agamemnon's side when you should be taking mine. You should hate the man who hates me for fear that my love for you may turn to hate." Then he gestured to Patroclus to make up the old man's bed.

Telamonian Ajax took the hint. "Let us go back, Odysseus," he said just as bluntly, "and give the assembly Achilles' answer — which is that he does not care enough for any of us to change his mind. Everyone accepts a blood-price, even for his own brother's death, but Achilles refuses for the sake of a girl."

For answer, Achilles simply repeated that he would not help put an end to Hector's rampaging until such time as the

---

[31]

Aetolia was a district of west-central Greece. The most famous myth about Meleager was a prophecy that he would live for so long as a branch burning on the hearth at his birth was not burnt up, so his mother doused the flames and kept it safe until he later killed her brothers - at which she threw the branch back on the fire - another case of disastrously uncontrolled anger.

Trojans reached his own ships.[32] So the others left and reported to the council.

"What did he say?" Agamemnon implored. "Will he help us?"

"He refuses your gifts," Odysseus answered, "and threatens to take ship and sail for home tomorrow. Phoenix has stayed with him so that he can leave as well."

Diomedes of the great war-cry had the last word. "Son of Atreus, I with you had never appealed to him now, for all you have done is make an already over-proud man more stubborn still. Let us forget Achilles. Let him make up his own mind whether to stay or go without help from us. For our part, having eaten and drunk well, I suggest we make for our beds and be up and about early tomorrow morning – with you leading and encouraging us from the front."

All of them approving this speech, they poured libations and retired to sleep.

---

[32] There is a strong ethical element in Homer. We are meant to understand that Achilles in the wrong now, even if in the right before. He will now, as a result, bring catastrophe on himself and Patroclus.

Book 10

Unable to sleep, worry continually gnawing at him, Agamemnon kept looking out over the nearby Trojan camp fires and at last decided to rouse wise Nestor to ask his advice about what they should do. But even as he was putting on his armour to leave, his brother Menelaus arrived on a similar mission, so deciding to call a full council instead, he sent his brother to rouse Idomeneus and Ajax, waiting where they were just then when they returned for fear they might all miss each other in the dark. Finally he woke old Nestor and told him what they had decided, whereupon the old man suggested they wake Diomedes and the others as well while he himself dressed and woke Odysseus. All then made a tour of the sentry positions to check that those on watch were awake and alert.

So the chiefs met in conclave again, Meriones and Nestor's son[33] joining them. Nestor proposed that they send out a scout to spy on the enemy's positions, so Diomedes volunteered first, but then others did so as well, including both Ajaxes, Meriones, Menelaus and Odysseus. Afraid, though, that the young man might choose his impetuous brother, Agamemnon urged Diomedes to choose whoever he thought best without

---

[33] Presumably Thrasymedes rather than Antilochus (Nestor's other son) since Homer says he lends Diomedes a sword.

regard for rank, so he chose Odysseus, cleverest of them all and the one they all knew Athene loved best.

Odysseus responded simply by saying that they had better get moving since night was already well advanced, so Thrasymedes lent Diomedes his sword, Meriones lent Odysseus a bow, sword and boar's head helmet, and the two set off without delay in the direction of the Trojan fires. As they went, Athene sent an omen in the form of a harsh-crying heron, at which Odysseus made a heartfelt prayer that she love him more dearly that night than she ever loved him while Diomedes more formally recalled her help for his father Tydeus and promised her a heifer with gilded horns if she would only watch over them and bring them safely back.

Now while they were making their way towards the Trojan lines, Hector also called a council of chiefs at which he too asked if anyone would undertake a reconnaissance mission behind enemy lines, in his case to learn whether the Greeks intended fighting next day or sailing for home instead. He promised the pick of the enemies' chariots and horse teams as reward, and at that, Dolon, already a rich man, put himself forward on the understanding that he be awarded the chariot and horses of great Achilles. His terms being accepted, he threw on a grey wolf-skin cloak, took up his bow and spear and set off into the darkness. Diomedes and Odysseus soon spotted him though, but did not reveal themselves or go after him until he was well past them and they were in a position to cut off any attempt at escape. Only then did they chase him, Diomedes eventually stopping the panic-stricken man in his tracks with a spear-throw over his shoulder.

Finding his voice, Dolon promised them any ransom they wanted, claiming that Hector had hustled him into scouting with the promise of Achilles' chariot and horses as his reward.

Odysseus, though, calmed the man, asked about the disposition of Trojan forces and guards and soon learned all they wanted to know.

"Hector and his chiefs are by the barrow of Ilus," Dolon swore. "There is no guard set for the army as a whole, and only the Trojans themselves have pickets by their camp fires. Having no women or children of their own to protect, their allies are all fast asleep."

"Where are these allies?" Odysseus asked.

"The Carians are nearest the sea. Next to them are the Paeonians, Leleges, Caucones and Pelasgians. The Lycian, Mysian and Phrygian charioteers are billeted by Thymbra. But why do you want to know so much detail? If it's raiding you want, the Thracians have only just arrived and are all by themselves at the far end of the front. Their chief is Rhesus, whose horses are the best and biggest I have ever seen, whiter than snow and fast as the wind. His chariot is silver-chased and his armour huge and gold. What will you do with me – take me back to your ships or tie me up here while you test the truth of what I say?"

Diomedes scowled. 'There is only one way to make sure you will be no trouble to us, Dolon."

Then, even as the other's hand reached out for his chin to plead with him, Diomedes whipped off his head off with a swipe of the sword and stripped his body of its armour and weapons which Odysseus dedicated to Athene with a prayer for her safe guidance to where the Thracians slept. Then they hid their booty in a tamarisk bush, marked the spot and moved on until they came to the Thracians whom they found sleeping beside their horses and armour. While Odysseus identified Rhesus in the middle of the group and set about harnessing his horses, Diomedes killed twelve of his men with the sword, followed by Rhesus himself. Athene herself had to dissuade him for being too greedy and killing still more. Other gods might wake the Trojans, she warned, so recognising her, Diomedes immediately jumped up into the chariot beside Odysseus who whipped up the horses with his bow. The two were soon back at the tamarisk bush where Diomedes retrieved the spoils of Dolon.

Old Nestor himself was first to hear the thunder of approaching hooves through the darkness and welcomed them. They gave him and the other chiefs an account of all they had done, after which they washed the blood and sweat from their bodies in the sea, bathed and oiled themselves properly and sat down to a late well-earned supper with plenty of sweet-hearted wine.

Book 11

As dawn rose and left Tithonus's bed,[34] Zeus sent down the dread goddess Hate to stand in the middle of the Greek ships from where she could be heard from end to end of the line, goading the Greeks into fierce hunger for fighting rather than a voyage home.

Agamemnon himself put on the silver-fastened leg and chest armour that Cinyras of Cyprus had given him to go to the war, then his silver-scabbarded sword and shield with its image of the Gorgon in the centre. On his head he set his plumed helmet and took up two spears. Hector, Polydamas and great Aeneas led the line against him, and the armies came together with a huge crash, delighting Hate,[35] the only one of the gods to attend that morning. The sides remained evenly balanced until, at that time of day when a tired woodcutter among the mountain glens might think of making his supper, the Trojans finally broke. First Agamemnon killed

---

34

See notes at end for Eos (the dawn) who asked Zeus to give her lover Tithonus immortality - but forgot to ask for eternal youth as well, so that he just got older and older ... and smaller and more shrivelled. (Cf the Struldbrugs in *The WCC Gulliver's Travels*).

35

Although personified as a god(dess), Hate, or Strife - the "lady of sorrows" - is an embodied idea like Lady Luck.

Bienor and Oileus, then Isus and Antiphus, both of them sons of Priam, stripping them of their armour. Next he dropped Peisander and Hippolochus who pleaded for mercy in exchange for a ransom – without success.

The next day, Agamemnon destroyed Trojans like a forest fire roared on by the wind, pushing them right back past Ilus's Barrow to the Scaean Gate where Zeus ordered Iris to tell Hector he might counter-attack as soon as he saw the Greek chief wounded. This Iris duly did, but for a while Agamemnon continued his slaughtering. First missing him with his spear, the Greek chief stabbed Antenor's son Iphidamas, then killed Coön[36] — who, though, first wounded him with a spear-thrust through the forearm. With blood running down him, Agamemnon raged on for a while but eventually had to withdraw, seeing which Hector counter-attacked as he had been told by the war-god, killing Asaeus, Autonous and Opites, then Dolops, Opheltius, Agelaus, Aesymnus, Orus and Hipponous.

Watching a rout unfold that looked likely to push them back to their ships again, Odysseus and Diomedes then called to each other and rallied the Greeks. Diomedes killed Thymbraeus, and Odysseus killed the man's companion Molion followed by Hippodamas and Hypeirochus. Next he speared Agastrophus in the hip as the man rushed impetuously forward, having abandoned the safety of his chariot – seeing which Hector stormed towards him with

---

[36]

The point of the odd 'ö' in this transliteration is that it denotes a separate vowel sound. The man is pronounced like 'go-on' rather than 'goon'.

reinforcements. Diomedes, though, aimed a spear that hit the Trojan full on the helmet, stunning him without penetrating the skull, so that he had to withdraw in his chariot. Exulting, Diomedes set about stripping armour from the dead Agostrophus — but as he did so, Paris pinned his foot to the ground with an arrow so that Odysseus had to free him for his charioteer to take back to the ships.

That left Odysseus alone of the great Greeks on that sector of the front, but although realising his danger, he fought on regardless. First he speared Deïopites in the shoulder, then Thoön, Ennomus and Chersidamas as he jumped out of his chariot. Without pausing, he went on to kill Charops, brother of the rich Socus who tried to rush him.

"Odysseus, famous schemer and adventurer," this last man called, "today you will either boast of killing both of Hipassus's sons — or yourself be killed by the survivor."

Socus's great spear crashed through Odysseus's shield and corslet, ripping into the flesh covering his ribs, but Athene kept the blow from his vitals so that, realising as much, he still had strength and conviction enough to drive his own spear between Socus's fleeing shoulders. Pulling the other's spear from his own body, his blood flowed so freely that the Trojans were inspired to renew their assault. Just in time, though, seeing the danger he was in, Menelaus and Telemonian Ajax ran up, Ajax holding off the Trojans while Agamemnon rescued the man himself. There Ajax killed Doryclus, Pandocus, Lysander, Pyrasus and Pylartes. Like some flash-flooding river out of the mountains he stormed across the plain, littering it with Trojan dead while Hector, now recovered, confronted Idomeneus and Peleus by the River Scamander. There Machaon, the great healer as well as great captain, was hit by one of Paris's arrows in the shoulder and had to be helped back to the ships by Nestor. Now, too, Hector careered off across Greek armour and bodies in a chariot whipped up by Cebriones, splashed by blood at every turn and still making for Ajax. Seeing him, the Greek hero had to retreat, although turning often to maul his pursuers.

The Greek Eurypylus arriving with two helpers then killed Apision with a spear in the liver, but as he bent forward to strip the armour from his body, Paris hit him with an arrow in the thigh so that he too had to retire from the fighting. Still, he had done his job, for the Greeks had been given time to form a line to protect Ajax, who in turn was able to make another stand.

By now they were all so close to the Greek camp that Achilles could watch events from the stern of his ship. Calling Patroclus, he asked him to check that the wounded chief he had seen Nestor carrying from the battle was indeed Machaon, thinking that he might be but wanting to be sure. So Patroclus made his way to the old man's tent where Nestor's slave Hecamede from Tenedos laid a table in front of the old hero and his companion Eurymedon, loading it with bread, honey and onions along with a giant drinking cup in which were Pramnian wine[37] mixed with grated goat's cheese and white barley. Seeing Patroclus, he offered him hospitality as well, but Patroclus refused.

"I am only here to find out who you brought back wounded," he said, "but I can see now it was Machaon."

---

[37]

A sweet, powerful and long-lived wine from Lesbos. Greek cuisine does not sound too appetising though.

"Did Achilles send you?" Nestor asked. "If so, why is he suddenly so concerned about the Greeks now that the best of us are all wounded? Diomedes has been hit by an arrow, Odysseus and Agamemnon have been stabbed by spears. Eurypylus and Machaon are bow-shot. Is he waiting for us all to be killed? How I wish I was young and strong again, as I was in a quarrel over cattle many years ago when I killed Hypeirochus.[38] My father Neleus was glad to share the booty out since until then we had had the worst of it in a war with Heracles and lost many of our best fighters — me being the only survivor of his twelve sons. As a result, the Epeans had taken to robbing us with impunity. Neleus himself had recently lost a chariot and horses that were on their way to a race, our enemy Augeas sending back only the driver. Now they returned to the attack, besieging our hill-town of Thryoessa, so we joined battle with them by a river and scattered them over the plain, me killing their best men, after which our men glorified Zeus first of all and then me. Achilles, though, is determined to nurse his courage in solitude for ever. But then you know all this, Patroclus, for that day when Odysseus and I came to Neleus's palace to take you and Achilles to the war, your own father gave you your orders. 'Achilles is older and stronger than you,' he said, 'so it must be your job to give him good advice.' Even now you could persuade him if you tried. Or if he will not himself

---

[38] Garrulous old Nestor narrates yet another heroic episode - some ninety lines in the Greek original - meant to have the effect all heroic story-telling, which was to inspire the hearer (or in this case Patroclus) to want to emulate the feats described.

fight, he might at least let you show yourself with his Myrmidons and perhaps save the ships."

On his way back, his head full of thoughts and pity, Patroclus caught sight of the wounded Eurypylus. "Eurypylus," he asked, "do you think the Greeks can hold out much longer against Hector and his Trojans?"

The other shook his head. "Without Achilles' help we are done for — but now help me get this arrow out of my leg since Machaon the healer is in need of healing himself."

So Patroclus, anxious though he was to get back to Achilles, helped the wounded man back to his ship where they cut the arrow barb from his thigh, staunching the blood and applying healing and pain-relieving herbs.

Book 12

Because they had not sacrificed or prayed to the gods for support, the Greek wall could not last. Still, for so long as Hector lived, Achilles remained angry and Troy untaken, for so long would it hold out. Once the war was over, though, and all those still alive had returned to their homes, Poseidon and Apollo would unleash huge storms to flood the rivers of the plain and wash it into the sea, leaving no sign that it ever existed.

But now Hector raged furiously all around it, trying to get in. Polydamas advised him not to attempt an assault with chariots. "Better," he said, "to leave them on this side of the ditch and advance on foot, lest the horses be injured by the sharpened stakes at the ditch bottom or the Greeks counter-attack us where there is least room for manoeuvre."

So the Trojan leader accepted his advice and formed the army into five divisions, one led by himself, the others by Paris, Helenus, Aeneas and Sarpedon together with their chief lieutenants. Asius, son of Hyrtacus and a leader in Helenus's command, disagreed with such caution though and drove on alone. Destined to be killed by Cretan Idomeneus, he made for the wall's left and crossed the ditch by a causeway still open there – but found Peirithous and Polypoites confronting him. Thus the battle raged, the air grew thick with missiles and men died.

Meanwhile, high in the sky over the main army, an eagle appeared carrying in its talons a huge red snake which, by no means dead, kept striking up at its raptor's head and neck until the bird was forced to drop it. Seeing this omen, Polydamas changed his advice.

"Hector," he urged, "the omen we have just seen, sent by Zeus, is a warning that even if we succeed in crossing the ditch and breaking the Greek's gate and wall, the enemy will counter-attack and cause us heavy losses."

This time, though, Hector was less than pleased. "Polydamas," he said, "you make no sense. Zeus himself has promised me the victory, and I am not interested in birds and snakes. Keep your opinions to yourself if you know what is good for you."[39]

So he urged the Trojans across, but stiffened by the two Ajaxes, the Greeks fought back hard, and soon the air was as full of missiles thrown by both sides as the sky is of snowflakes when Zeus sends a blizzard to mask and muffle in turn mountains, meadows, harbours and even the sea itself. But Sarpedon finally made a breakthrough. "Glaucus," he shouted to his companion, "throughout our lives, we have been honoured almost as gods by our people, the Lycians. Now it is time to earn what we have been given. What point is there in hanging back from the fighting anyway? However

---

[39]

As part of a general tendency to place a moralistic construction on events, events disastrous for the Trojans are increasingly made their fault, even though they are also fated. So far, for example, Hector has been the model dutiful defender ("I have learned to be brave"), but more and more, he becomes over-confident, his judgement flawed.

long a man lives, he cannot put off death for ever. Better, then, to play for glory."[40]

He and his Lycians attacked. Glaucus was soon wounded by an arrow in the arm, but Sarpedon himself fought on and demolished a whole stretch of battlements with his bare hands - through which breach his Lycians poured. For a while the balance of violence remained poised, but now Zeus gave the day to the Trojans. Encouraging his men even harder, Hector himself picked up a boulder heavier than any two men could lift nowadays and with it smashed in the gates of the wall. Huge as they were, they gave way. He burst through - and now the Greeks scattered in terror among their ships.

---

[40]

This famous speech sums up the Homeric heroic ethos:

Book 13

Now, while Hector and the Trojans drove on among the ships, Zeus turned his eyes and mind to other matters, but Poseidon the Earth-shaker, still watching from a peak on Samos,[41] pitied the Greeks and resented what he saw his brother doing to them. Defiant, giant-striding, he now went down to his golden palace under the sea, dressed in golden robes, took up his spears, harnessed horses to his chariot and skimmed the foam to an undersea cave off Troy where he left the team and came ashore.

Disguised as the seer Calchas, he first of all whipped up the morale of the two Ajaxes, then that of other chief Greeks who were resting, urging them on. In the crash of forces that followed, Hector's attack was held at the ships while Deiphobus was stopped by Meriones. Meanwhile Teucer killed Imbrius and Hector killed Amphimachus, even though Telamonian Ajax prevented him from stripping the body. Still stirring up the Greeks, Poseidon next came across Cretan Idomeneus who was just then returning from helping a comrade away for treatment. Disguised as Thoas, he urged him back into the fighting, but while on his way to do so, the

---

41

Modern Samothrace, the island of Samos in the north Aegean, Sea where the famous Nike, or Winged Victory, was found in 1863.

man met Meriones returning to his quarters to fetch a replacement spear for one he had just broken on Deiphobus.

"There are spares in my quarters which are closer than yours," Idomeneus told him. "Take one of those."

So Meriones did, catching up with the other again soon afterwards.

"Where do think we should lend our weight?" he asked the Cretan chief. "To me, our left looks weakest."

"The Ajaxes and Teucer can hold the centre," Idomeneus agreed. "So let us make for the left as you suggest."

They then sped to the battle near the ships' sterns where all was confusion like a blinding storm that had whipped up dust devils. Idomeneus first killed Othryoneus who had come to Troy to win Priam's daughter Cassandra by his fighting, then Asius who tried to prevent him from stripping the body of its armour. The man fell like a huge oak or pine tree and died roaring and scrabbling at the bloody dust in front of him. Grieving for him, Deiphobus made for Idomeneus with his spear - but killed Hypsenor instead.

Soon Idomeneus was unstoppable. He killed Alcathous next while Poseidon held the man in a trance and jeered at Deiphobus who had killed only one man to his three, daring the other to take him on. Deiphobus considered it but decided first to get the help of Aeneas who, angry over the death of his brother-in-law Alcathous, joined him – whereupon both sides called for reinforcements, Aeneas and Deiphobus bringing up Paris and Agenor while Idomeneus and Meriones brought up Ascalephus, Deipyrus and Antilochus.

Now the battle roared even higher. Aeneas aimed his spear at Idomeneus but missed. Idomeneus killed Oenomaus but could not strip him of his armour in the crush. Next it was

Deiphobus's turn to miss. He hit Ascalephus instead, but even as he tore the helmet from the man's head, Meriones speared him through the arm so that he had to drop his spoils and be helped out of the action back to Troy.

Next Aeneas killed Alphareus with a spear in the throat, Nestor's son Antilochus killed Thoön while Adamas, Asius's son, died the harshest of all battle deaths as Meriones' spear took him between the navel and the genitals. Then, after Helenus had killed Deipyrus, Menelaus joined in once more for the Greeks, wounding him in the hand so that Agenor had to help him away as well. Now Peisandrus and Menelaus tore into each other. Both missed with their spears, so both drew other weapons and struck at the same moment, Peisandrus with an axe to the other's helmet, Menelaus with his sword. Peisandrus fell while Menelaus cursed the Trojans for their battle-greediness as he stripped the man's armour. Meanwhile Meriones hit Harpalion with an arrow in the buttock and bladder after the other had lunged at Menelaus with his spear, so Paris in revenge aimed at Euchenor, a rich Corinthian who preferred to die fighting Trojans than from a painful disease at home (those being the choices he knew he faced), hitting him between jaw and ear.

Now while all this was happening on the left of the line, Hector fought in the centre, unstopped by the Greeks. The two Ajaxes continued to resist him, though, the lesser Ajax's Locrians causing such carnage with their slingshots that Polydamas made so bold as to advise Hector again, this time suggesting that the Trojans re-group with the aim of bringing in some of their men now resting and concentrating their best fighters where they were most needed. He also took the opportunity to warn the Trojan chief that they were dangerously near the quarters of Achilles and his Myrmidons who were unlikely to stay out of the battle very much longer.

Approving his caution this time, Hector paused in his fighting to look for Deiphobus, Helenus, Adamas, Asios and the others but found only his brother Paris, who told him some were dead while others were wounded and out of action. Re-grouping, then, Hector pressed on. Spotting him, Telemonian Ajax promised him a beating — while he in turn promised Ajax an even bigger one,[42] and so the battle raged on at, if possible, yet greater pitch.

---

[42]

Bragging is common and necessary in heroic poetry. With combat so close, violent and personal, fighters needed to demoralise their enemy and build up their own confidence by all available means. Look at any two boxers at a televised weigh-in.

Book 14

As the uproar of battle got closer, Nestor in his quarters rose in alarm and told Machaon to stay where he was having his wounds dressed while he himself went out to see what was going on. Taking up his spear and shield, he left and found the turmoil so brutal that for a while he felt as buffeted as a wild sea at the beginning of a storm, unsure whether to join in the fighting or to look for Agamemnon. He chose the second course and soon came across the wounded chief with Diomedes and Odysseus advancing from the shore behind, the Greek ships being so many that they had been dragged out of the water and beached in rows.

"Are matters then so bad?" Agamemnon asked in despair. "Now I begin to think there must be other Greeks apart from Achilles who no longer want to fight for me and that Hector will overwhelm us as he threatened."

"It is the will of Zeus," Nestor told him. "Our ditch and wall are both now fallen."

"Then we are finished. We must drag the ships down to the water and moor them offshore so that everyone can go aboard and sail when the day's battle is over."

"Atreus's son, you are mad?" Odysseus interrupted forcefully. "Do you seriously suggest we abandon Troy after enduring so much for so long in the effort to take her? Can you imagine your own soldiers wanting to fight on even throughout today if, in the middle of their fighting, they looked over their shoulder to see you lugging ships down to the water?"

"You are right, Odysseus, however rough your words," Agamemnon had to admit, "but do you, or anyone else, have a better suggestion?"

"Yes," Diomedes answered at once. "Young as I am, I come from a line of great fighters, so do not put me down by saying I am not worth listening to. Although we ourselves cannot fight on, wounded as we are, we can at least lead and encourage, letting the men on both sides see us. Our troops will then take heart — while theirs will think twice before getting too close."

The others agreeing with him, the wounded chiefs limped off painfully towards the carnage again, and as they did so, Poseidon in the guise of an old man took Agamemnon by the hand.

"Great king, Achilles may be pleased to see the disasters that have struck you, but do not imagine the gods have either forgotten or abandoned you." He then suddenly left them with a huge roar that heartened all and attracted the attention of Hera who recognised him and was delighted that at least one god, who was both her brother and brother-in-law[43], supported her favourites. Thinking how she might help as well, it occurred to her to seduce her husband, fill him with the urge to lie with her naked so that afterwards he might fall asleep, overcome by love and tiredness, for a while unaware of what was going on in the waking world. So she went to her

---

[43]

See the list of characters at the end for the often complicated physical relations between and among gods!

79

room, bathed, combed her hair, perfumed her beautiful body, dressed herself gorgeously and visited Aphrodite.

"Lend me beauty and desire," she asked the other. "I am on my way to visit old Ocean, ancestor of the gods, and ancient Tethys who once looked after me like a mother. They have been estranged from each other for so long that they no longer even share a bed. I want them to desire each other again and be reconciled."

So laughing Aphrodite lent her the immortal girdle she wore beneath her breasts on which are embroidered all those seductive charms and soft words that make fools of even the wisest men. Hera took it and sped down from Olympus, crossing snowy-mountained Thrace until she came to the island of Lemnos where she called on Sleep, Death's brother, and begged him to lull Zeus into dreamland for her sake. On being promised as a reward the nymph Pasithea whom he had long fancied, Sleep agreed, and so these two hid themselves in a mist and came to Ida,[44] mother of wild beasts, where Sleep perched in the top of a pine tree disguised as the little bird called 'bronze-throat' by the gods.[45] Hera, though, went on further, to the peak of Gargarus where Zeus saw her and was suddenly as overcome by desire as that first time when they made love without their parents' knowledge. Asking why she

---

[44]

A mountain range in the southern Troad (the ancient region of which Troy was the capital) - but also a mountain in Crete where Zeus was thought to have been born.

[45]

Possibly the nightjar, the male of which woodland species makes a strange whirring call while incubating eggs.

had come, he was given the answer she had already given Aphrodite.

'Well never mind that now," he said. "Never in my life have I so wanted a woman — no, not Ixion's wife, nor Danaë, Europa, Semele, Alcmene, Demeter or the incomparable Leto— as much as I now want you. Come and lie with me."

"On the flanks of Ida, wide open to the sky?" Hera asked, innocently scandalized. "Can't you wait to be more private in our bedroom?"

For answer, Zeus made a golden cloud which he drifted about them so that no eye could penetrate inside or see what they were up to. There he enjoyed her, there the earth beneath them bloomed with fresh grass, lotus blossom, crocuses and hyacinths, and when his love-making was over, he lay in his wife's arms, pole-axed by sleep — whereupon Sleep himself ran to the Greek ships to tell Poseidon that for a while he was free to do what he wanted in the battle. So the Earth-shaker sprang out in front of the Greeks and called out in a huge voice, stiffening their resolve.

"You Greeks, put your best arms and armour on your best fighters, put them in the front of the fighting and stiffen your own resolve. With me leading you, not even Hector will be able to stand up to you for long."

So they did as he commanded, the wounded chiefs marshalling their men and ordering those with the best gear to give it to the best fighters. Now too Hector marshalled his Trojans, and the two sides met with even greater fury than before, crashing against each other with a sound like surf on a beach when the wind blows really hard from the north - greater than the roar of forest fires or gales through oak tree boughs.

First Hector hit Ajax with his spear — but it did not penetrate to the man himself who in reply hit him with a rock to the top of his chest so hard that he fell and had to be carried out of the fighting, being brought round momentarily by the waters of Xanthus, only to pass out again after coughing up blood.

Their spirits lifting as they saw him leave, the Greeks then attacked the harder. Oïlean Ajax killed Satnius, at which, in revenge, Polydamas drove his spear through Prothoënor's shoulder - at which, again in revenge, the greater Ajax threw at him but missed, killing Archelochus instead. Acamas, the fallen man's brother, then stabbed Promachus who was trying to drag the body off but had to dodge a charge by Penelaus who hit Ilioneus instead, he whom the god Hermes loved best of all the Trojans, catching him just under the eye, gouging it clean out and shearing through the tendons of his neck. Even as the man died, Penelaos hacked his head off and held it up on his spear-point with one eyeball still impaled on its end.

Now the Earth-shaker reversed the fortune of battle. Telamonian Ajax cut down Hyrtius, Antilochus killed Phalces and Mermerus, while Meriones cut down Morys and Hippotion and Teucer did the same for Prothoön and Periphetes. Menelaus meanwhile spilt the guts of Hyperenor, but no-one was able to kill faster than Ajax, son of Oïleus, since no-one was faster or deadlier on men running away.

Book 15

When Zeus awoke, saw the Trojans pushed back beyond the ditch and wall, Poseidon helping the Greeks and Hector dazed and vomiting blood, he guessed what had happened and came close to violence towards his wife Hera who in fear swore the strongest oaths a god could swear that she had done nothing to encourage the Earth-shaker.[46] Simmering down, Zeus sent her to Olympus with orders to send Iris and Apollo to him, the archer-god's mission being to heal and strengthen Hector so that he could return to the fighting and push the Greeks back to their ships. There, he added, Patroclus would be inspired to kill many Trojans in revenge – even his own son Sarpedon[47] – until Hector in turn killed him. Achilles would then rejoin the fighting and kill Hector, after which the war would swing decisively the Greeks' way and Troy at last fall. Until Achilles'

---

[46]

Disconcertingly, Homer's gods not only flirt, seduce and are capable of most human vices, plus a few, but can also be economical with the truth. Since Hera relayed her plot to Poseidon only by way of the god of Sleep, she is technically not lying!

[47]

Here is the clearest expression of the relations between fate, divinity and free will. As implied in the note above, it is their *power* that mainly distinguishes gods from men - yet even Zeus who determines the course of the war cannot save his son who is fated to die - or could, but the result would be moral and physical catastrophe for the world (*see* next book).

prayer had been answered according to the promise he had made to Thetis, though, no help was to be given the Greeks.

So Hera fled to Olympus from the mountains of Ida where, meeting the other gods in assembly, she accepted a welcoming cup from Themis and told them they were mad to oppose Zeus.

"Your own fighting," she pointed out to Ares, "is the reason why your own son Ascalaphus has just lost his life to the Trojans."

Furious at that news, not having heard it until then, the war god leapt up and ordered Fear and Terror to harness his horses, bent on revenge. Athene, though, followed and reasoned with him while Hera gave Iris the message that Zeus wanted conveyed to Poseidon, which was that he was to withdraw from the fighting immediately or face the weight of his brother's anger. Iris did as she was asked, and it was then the Earth-shaker's turn to be infuriated.

"Why should I, Zeus's equal with Hades since we three were born brothers to Rhea and Cronos, meekly do what he orders?" he demanded. "The earth is common to all three of us,[48] so I will go my own way." Iris, though, urged restraint, reminding him that the Furies usually sided with the elder of the family in a quarrel, so he reconsidered and smiled at her. "You are right," he said. "Very well. I will give way this time — but if Troy does not fall soon and the Greeks gain the victory, there will be a serious falling-out between us."

---

[48] According to myth, the sons of Cronos divided their father's realm: Zeus ruled the sky, Poseidon the sea, Hades the Underworld - the earth being common to all three. *(See note on the Furies too).*

So he returned to the sea while Zeus sent Apollo to heal and breathe new strength into Hector and panic into the Greeks until they fled back to the ships and the narrows of Helle.[49] So the god did all this, and Hector responded like a war-horse set free or a stag driven by hunters. Now Thoas, son of Andraemon, proposed an orderly Greek retreat which the Greeks agreed to, but as arrows jumped from bows, spears flew and Apollo stared into their eyes, they panicked instead and ran. In the confusion Hector killed Boeotian Arcesilaus and Stichius while Aeneas killed Medon, half-brother of the lesser Ajax, and Iasus. Polydamas killed Mecisteus, Polites Echius, while Agenor cut down Clonius. Paris, too, downed his man, Deiochus, who had turned to run, taking his spear in his back. It passed clean through him.

Now while these paused to strip their victims' armour from them, Hector roared on the others, threatening to kill anyone who held off from harrying Greeks, and so the Trojans, aided by Apollo who easily flattened the ditch and wall for them, were able to push their enemies right back to the ships once more. Now the assault surged again around these like waves of a sea-storm, resisted only by those Greeks who, having retreated aboard, thrust at their attackers with the long pikes they used for sea-fighting.

And now, watching it all from close up where he was still dressing Eurypylus's wounds, unable to stand the sight any longer, Patroclus suddenly abandoned his patient to his own

---

[49]

Helle was one of two mythical children transported across the sea on a winged golden ram. Where she fell, the waters are still named after her: Hellespont = Helles' Sea.

helpers and ran back to Achilles in hopes that he might even now be able to rouse the great chief to come to the Greeks' defence. Meanwhile Hector made for Telamonian Ajax on board his ship, but neither man could force a conclusion, although Ajax killed Caletor with a spear-thrust as he was carrying fire to his ship - at which Hector threw but hit Ajax's follower, Lycophron, below the ear, toppling him from the vessel's high stern.

Now Ajax called on Teucer to use the bow Apollo had given him. So Teucer did, aiming at Cleitus, one of Polydamas's lieutenants who was just then managing a charging chariot and team, hitting him in the neck. Next he aimed at Hector himself, but Zeus snapped his bow-string, making the weapon useless. Now both Hector and Ajax breathed fire and courage into their respective troops' hearts, and Hector killed Schedus, a son of Perimides, while Ajax killed Laodamas and Polydamas killed Cyllenian Otus. Distraught at this last, Otus's friend Meges lunged at Polydamas in revenge – but caught Croesmus full in the chest instead. As he bent to strip his armour though, he himself was charged by Dolops whose spear smashed clean through his shield but failed to pierce his body armour. Once more both men went for each other, but the unlucky Dolops did not spot Menelaus coming from behind to kill him. At that, Hector called on Melanippus to avenge his cousin while, egged on by Menelaus, Antilochus made a bid for glory as well, leaping out from the Greek ranks to kill Menalippus as he advanced – before retreating again before Hector's charge.

As the Trojans threw themselves at the Greek ships, Zeus continued to refuse mercy or help to the Greeks until he had made good his promise and seen fire lift from their vessels' hulls, and so the battle raged on, waves of Trojans pouring over the leading line of beached vessels like breakers, forcing the defenders back to their huts and quarters – all except Telamonian Ajax who still strode up and down his deck, whirling his mighty sea-pike. Now Protesilaus's[50] ship became the focus of fierce combat, Greeks and Trojans contesting it so hotly and at such close quarters that they had to use axes and swords on each other instead of spears and arrows. Now Hector gripped the vessel's stern and refused to let go of it while Ajax retreated to its midships section where, expecting to die at any moment, he continued swinging his sea-pike to great effect, wounding twelve men.

---

[50] Protesilaus was the first of the Greeks to be killed when the arriving fleet first beached (*see* Book 2). A deliberate irony.

Book 16

Weeping like baby begging to be picked up, or a grown man bearing the worst possible news, Patroclus came to Achilles.

"Diomedes has been hit by an arrow," he told the other. "Odysseus and Agamemnon both carry spear wounds and Eurypylus has an arrow in his thigh. The Greeks are being destroyed while you do nothing. Rocks and stones bred you, Achilles, not Peleus and Thetis. If you cannot forget your anger, at least let me put on your armour and lead the Myrmidons. The Trojans might then think you have rejoined the fighting and break off their attack."

"I am not heartless," Achilles told him. "It is just that I cannot forget how a man no more than my equal took from me a girl I won with my own spear and the army awarded me as my prize of honour. For that I swore I would not rejoin the fighting until it reached my ships. You, though, may put on my armour and lead my Myrmidons — on condition that you only lift the immediate danger and compel the Greeks to give back the beautiful girl they stole from me. Do not, that is, go further and follow the Trojans over the plain towards their city, for that would diminish my glory and perhaps cost you your life."

While they spoke Ajax at last had to give up the defence of his ship. The sweat pouring off him, his helmet and armour rang from their continual battering — and now Hector's sword sliced off the head of his pike. Even as he withdrew, flames engulfed the ship, at which Achilles slapped his thigh and urged Patroclus forward. So the other put on Achilles' armour and took up two spears while Automedon harnessed the horses, two of which were divine beasts sired by the West Wind out of Podarge, a thoroughbred that Achilles had captured in war. As he did so, Achilles readied the Myrmidons, deploying them in five divisions, the first led by Menestheus,[51] son of the river Spercheus and the beautiful Polydora, the other four by Eudorus, Peisander, old Phoenix and Alcimedon.

"Now you can all do what you have been dreaming of," he told them when they were drawn up. "Don't think I don't know the names you have been calling me behind my back. Now you have work to do — so go to it like brave men."

He returned to his quarters and unpacked a goblet used by him alone to pour drink offerings to almighty Zeus. Cleaning and filling it, he prayed in his courtyard, first that Patroclus and his Myrmidons might drive the Trojans from the ships, second that Patroclus might return safe from the battle, but while granting the first prayer, Zeus would not grant the second.

Now the Myrmidons charged like wasps poked unwisely out of their nest by small boys, and the sight of them alone, led by a figure who certainly looked like Achilles, panicked the Trojans into retreat. Now Patroclus killed Pyraechmes by Protesilaus's ship, drove the man's followers from the vessel and doused the flames. And now, seeing that they had been reinforced, the other Greeks broke out from behind their ships like a mountain flash flood sent by Zeus to scour men's sins.

----

[51]

Not the Menestheus killed by Paris in Book 7.

Now Patroclus hit Areilycus in the thigh with his spear, smashing the bone, while Menelaus killed Thoas,[52] Meges picked off the charging Amphiclus and Nestor's son Antilochus killed Atymnius. The dead man's brother lunged at Antilochus, determined to have revenge, but Thrasymedes killed him with a sword thrust, shearing off his arm at the base.

Now, too, the lesser Ajax caught and killed Cleobolus, and Penelaos almost severed the head of Lycon after both had missed with their spears. Meriones speared Acamas as he tried to climb up behind his horses, and Idomeneus stabbed Erymas in the mouth so that his teeth flew out and he blew a brief spray of blood through his nose.

Seeing the Greeks killing so freely, Hector led the retreat, scudding back across the plain and leaving many Trojans trapped in the ditch behind the wall where their chariot shafts had been shattered. Then Patroclus followed across the plain to get at him, determined to cut off the retreat of the Trojans before they could seek shelter inside their city. First he killed Pronous, then Thestor who huddled unnerved and terrified in the bottom of his chariot, stabbing him through the side of the head and afterwards hooking him out the way a man gaffs a fish into his boat. Next he killed the onrushing Erylaus with a stone, then Erymas, Tlepolemus, Amphoterus, Epaltes, Echius and Pyris, Ipheus, Euippus and Polemelus.

Noting all this, Sarpedon rallied his Lycians and counterattacked, at which Zeus wept, watching. "It is hard to accept my son's destiny, which is to die at the hands of

---

[52]

Not the son of Andraemon, one of the important younger Greek chiefs *(see Book 15).*

Patroclus," he groaned. "Even now I am inclined to snatch him from battle and set him down safe in far-away Lycia."

"Son of Cronos," answered his wife, "you cannot mean to set destiny aside by rescuing a man doomed to die. If you do, every other god will want to do the same, for they all have loved favourites. No – however much you cherish your Sarpedon, let him die. But afterwards let Sleep and Death carry him to Lycia where his brothers and fellow-countrymen can bury him with ceremony and honour."[53]

So, weeping tears of blood, Zeus gave way. Noting Sarpedon's approach, Patroclus threw first, hitting the other's charioteer, Thrasymedes, in the lower belly. Then Sarpedon threw, killing Padasus, the third of Patroclus's horses. Sawing at the animals' harness with his sword, the charioteer Automedon cut the other two beasts free, while Patroclus then threw a second time, hitting Sarpedon in the solar plexus next to the heart. The great Lycian fell like a huge poplar or pine, shouting aloud in his agony.

"Now, Glaucus, you must rescue my body," he screamed, "or face the shame of seeing my armour stripped before your eyes."

So he died. Patroclus, planting his heel on his chest to pull his spear out, yanked the whole midriff out, but Glaucus was helpless to intervene because of the wound he had taken from Teucer's arrow. Instead he prayed to Apollo who deadened the pain and strengthened him so that he could run to Hector with the news. In fury and sorrow, the Trojans ran to prevent the Greeks from stripping Sarpedon's body, and now Hector killed

---

[53] Homer's somehow reconciles unalterable fate with divine free will by suggesting that Zeus voluntarily accepts it - while also, perhaps, reconciling one traditional story of Sarpedon's death at Troy with another about him having a tomb in Lycia.

Epeigeus, smashing his skull in with a stone while Patroclus did the same to Sthenelaos. It was the Trojans, Hector included, who gave way first though, but not before Glaucus had killed Bathycles and Meriones had retaliated by killing Laogonus. Aeneas threw at Meriones, missing, and now men swarmed all around Sarpedon's body like flies around a milk pail while Zeus pondered whether Patroclus should die there and then or after driving the Trojans back to their city and so winning more glory for himself.

Deciding on the second, he made a coward of Hector, who turned his chariot and bolted, shouting to the other Trojans to follow, and now at last the Greeks stripped Sarpedon's armour while Apollo, on Zeus's orders, snatched the body itself, washed it with ambrosia, wrapped it in a cloak and gave it to Sleep and Sleep's twin Death to carry off to his home in Lycia. Meanwhile Patroclus stormed on, killing Adrestus, Autonous and Echeclus, then Perimus, Epistor, Melanippus, Elasus, Mulius and Pylartes. Even high-gated Troy might have fallen to him. Three times he tried to climb its walls, and three times Apollo had to shove him back, warning him with a great yell when he tried yet again.

"Give way, Patroclus! It is not Troy's destiny to fall to your spear, or even to that of Achilles who is a much greater man than you!"

So Patroclus gave way as Hector, prompted by Apollo, counter-attacked from under the Scaean Gate, and now it was the turn of the Greeks to fall back— although not before Patroclus had killed Hector's charioteer Cebriones with a stone that stove in the man's forehead. He and Hector then fought over the body, and for a while the battle raged evenly. Once again, though, the Greeks gained a temporary upper hand and stripped the man of his armour. Three times Patroclus charged, each time cutting down nine men, but the fourth time was the end of him, for Apollo suddenly thumped him in the back, sending helmet, shield and spear spinning. Then, as he stood dazed, Euphorbus hit him in the shoulder with a javelin. Finally, as he tried to escape back into the Greek ranks, Hector was too fast for him and drove his spear deep into his belly.

"You thought to take Troy by yourself," he crowed over the dying man. "Now not even Achilles can save you."

"Don't think this is your victory, Hector," the other could still, just, answer. "You are only my third killer after Apollo and Euphorbus – and soon it will be your turn to die at Achilles' hands."

Then his soul fluttered free from its body. Meanwhile Hector went after Automedon with his spear, but the dead man's charioteer managed to escape with the immortal horses given to Peleus by the gods themselves.

Book 17

Menelaus straddled the body of Patroclus, shielding it like a cow its first-born calf.

"Give way, Menelaus," Euphorbus shouted, "or I will kill you too."

"You sons of Panthous are big talkers," Menelaus shouted back, "but small doers. Your brother Hyperenor called me the weakest of the Greeks, and he won't be going home to his wife and family either."[54]

So Euphorbus lunged, but his spear point bent back from Menelaus's shield while Menelaus's caught him in the gullet. The Greek chief pushed right through, killing the man outright, but while he stripped the other's body, as uncaring of the Trojans' attempts to dislodge him as a mountain lion of the shepherds' efforts to get him off its kill, Apollo came to Hector disguised as the Ciconian chief Mentes to tell him what had happened. Screaming hate and sorrow, Hector then closed on Menelaus, forcing him back, but now Menelaus called for help as well, bringing up Telamonian Ajax who was able to stop Hector from seizing the body of Patroclus, though not from stripping it of Achilles' armour.

Now it was Hector's turn to be forced to withdraw — only to be confronted by an angry Glaucus who accused him of cowardice and disloyalty to the Trojans' greatest ally and

---

[54] Killed by Menelaus at the end of Book 14.

threatened to withdraw his Lycians from the fighting. So Hector was shamed back to the struggle. First, though, he ran back to catch up with the men whom he had sent to Troy with Achilles' armour which he now put on. At this Zeus frowned and plotted his penalty from afar[55] yet permitted him further success for a while. Returning to the fighting then, Hector now roused his famous commanders: Mesthles and Glaucus, Thersilochus and Medon, Deisenor, Hippothous and Asteropaeus, Phorcys, Chromius and the bird-augurer Ennomus. Promising half the spoils and a full share of the glory to any man who could carry off the body of Patroclus, he led them into the struggle. But seeing them, Menelaus called for reinforcements as well, and there came running the lesser Ajax, Idomeneus and Meriones to stand beside him and Telamonian Ajax.

The Trojans charged, but the Greeks counter-attacked, dislodging them from Patroclus's body, Hippothous being killed by Telamonian Ajax as he tried to drag it off by a foot. Then Hector threw at Ajax but hit Schedius instead, best of the Phocians. In reply Ajax killed Phorcys, and now, as the Trojans gave way again, the Greeks stripped the bodies of those they had killed. Now, indeed, the Trojans might even have been forced back inside their city had not Apollo inspired Aeneas who killed Leiocritus. Pitying the fallen man, Lycomedes launched a spear in retaliation, hitting Apisaon, son of Hippasus, in the liver. Nor could Asteropaeus avenge Apisaon, for now the greater Ajax ranged men all round Patroclus's

---

[55] Perhaps a key moment in establishing the relation of fate to free will in the *Iliad*. Hector's putting on Achilles' armour suggests heroic arrogance that invites a fall already decided by Zeus and fate anyway.

body, forbidding any to break ranks. And so all fought on at close quarters until the ground ran with blood. Elsewhere men fought in sunlight, but here at the storm's centre, men sweated, struck and died in half-darkness, none fighting harder than Nestor's sons Thrasymedes and Antilochus who did not even know yet that Patroclus was dead. Neither side would give way.

At a distance from the fighting, the horses of Achilles stood motionless, heads down, mourning their dead master, so that Zeus himself pitied them.

"It was cruel to give immortal horses to mortal men, saddest of all the creatures that live on earth," he said. "Still, you must carry Automedon for a while as I continue to give glory to the Trojans."

So he breathed fresh power into them and they returned to the fighting, even though Automedon could not take part since he was busy managing them and the chariot until Alcimedon jumped up and took the reins while he got down to wield weapons. Seeing Achilles' divine team in action again, Hector and Aeneas once more tried to capture it, but seeing them approach, Automedon called to the Ajaxes and Menelaus while he himself threw at, and killed, a Trojan called Aretus whose armour he stripped while the Ajaxes fended off Hector and Aeneas.

Meanwhile Athene inspired Menelaus to kill Podes, a rich and good man as well as close friend of Hector who, given the news by Apollo, came running up. Now Idomeneus, on foot, was saved from his spear only by the arrival of Coeranus who galloped up — only to die instead as Hector's spear knocked out his teeth and cut his tongue in half. Meriones, though, managed to gather up the reins and advised Idomeneus to whip up the horses and make for the ships since it was now clear that the Trojans were once more wresting the advantage.

But great-hearted Ajax would not budge, concerned only that someone be sent back to Achilles with word of what had happened. Peering about in the gloom, he prayed to Zeus who cleared the mist from in front of him to show Menelaus whom he then asked to send Nestor's son Antilochus. Unwilling to move away from Patroclus's body to give the order, though, Menelaus did so after urging Meriones and the Ajaxes to fight the harder, whereupon he went searching for his son who, hearing of the disaster at last, stood rooted to the spot a long moment in grief. Menelaus told him to return and urge Achilles to rescue the body since Hector had already stripped it of its armour. Then he appointed Thrasymedes to marshal the Pylians in his brother's absence while he himself returned to the defence of the body. Arriving, he told the other chiefs what he had done but warned them there was little even Achilles would be able to do since he now had no armour. So Telamonian Ajax suggested that Menelaus and Meriones try to carry the body clear while he and Oïlean Ajax, who so often fought shoulder to shoulder, guarded their retreat.

When the Trojans saw the body being retrieved, they rushed forward like hounds after a wounded boar, only to stop and retire again every time the Ajaxes turned to confront them. Now the fighting was like the roar of flames in a burning city, its force that of man-made dykes that somehow manage to contain the strength of waters in spate. In this way, the Ajaxes kept their formation and protected the other chiefs' retreat while the younger fighters screamed in terror at the repeated swoops of Hector and Aeneas.

Book 18

Now Antilochus reached Achilles who, seeing the Trojans rampaging and the Greeks running away, had an inkling already of what the cause might be. When Antilochus confirmed it, he threw himself on the ground, covered himself with dust and tore his hair so that Antilochus had to seize him by the wrists for fear he might try to kill himself. Even in the depths of the sea where she sat with her father Nereus and her sisters — Glauce, Thaleia, Cymodoce, Nesaea, Speio, Thoë and ox-eyed Halie; Cymothoe, Actaee and Limnoreia, Melite, Iera, Amphithoe and Agaue; Doto, Pherusa, Dynamene, Dexamene, Amhinome and Callianeira; Doris, Panope and Galatea; Nemertes, Apseudes and Callinassa; Clymene with Ianeira, Ianassa, Maera, Oreithuia, lovely-haired Amatheia and all the other daughters of Nereus — his mother heard the terrible cry.[56]

"Hear me, sisters!" mourned Thetis, "I gave birth to a son who is tall and strong but destined for death and unhappiness." Then she and they came out of the sea and gathered around Achilles. She took his head in her arms and begged him to say why he was so troubled since Zeus had granted all he prayed for.

---

[56] Like the description of Achilles' shield later, this list of Nereus's (the Old Man of The Sea's) many beautiful daughters is meant to have a calming, hypnotic effect.

"Mother, I have lost my dearest friend whose life I loved as much as my own. Hector, who killed him, has also stripped my armour from his body. Now I no longer want to go home safe from the fighting if I cannot make Hector pay for what he has done."

"But if Hector dies, you die," his mother wailed, "for it is fated that your death must follow his."

"Then let it follow. I can never go back to the land of Patroclus's fathers anyway since I was not there to defend him but sitting here an idle and useless weight on the earth.[57] How I wish all anger that permeates men's being and becomes a drug they cannot live without would vanish from the earth. But it is too late for regrets. Now I must avenge Patroclus and accept my own death if that be the cost. There will be a time to lie quietly in earth. Now I must win glory."

Thetis accepted what he said. "Yes, my son, but first you must rescue your friends who are in danger. You have no armour. Do not stir then until I come back with new armour made by the armourer god Hephaestus."

So she sent her sisters to tell their father what had happened as she made her own way to Olympus. Meanwhile the Trojans roared on, approaching ever closer to the Greek ships. Three times Hector caught hold of the dead Patroclus's feet. Three times the Ajaxes fought him off but could not push him away. Now indeed they were likely to lose their struggle, but Iris, sent secretly by Hera, urged Achilles to show himself by the ramparts and ditch where the mere sight of him might terrify

---

[57] The mysterious relation of fate to free will partly explains the realisation (developed in later Greek tragedy) that while we may think we act as we choose - we often do not realize what we have chosen until too late.

the Trojans and put fresh heart in the Greeks. So Achilles did so while Athene draped her terrible aegis[58] round his powerful shoulders and set a gold shining cloud about his head like the beacons which a besieged city burns to warn the neighbouring islands that it is under attack. By the ditch he uttered his great war cry three times, each time routing the Trojans and causing twelve of them to die in panic on their own spears or under their own chariot wheels. Meanwhile the Greeks managed to retrieve the body of Patroclus and then at last the sun went down on all their sufferings.

Before making supper, the Trojans held a council at which Polydamas, who was better with words than Hector, although not so good with the spear, both men being born on the same night, urged withdrawal, suggesting that they spend the night inside Troy's walls in case Achilles rejoined the fighting and caught them out in the open. Hector, though, disagreed angrily.

"Polydamas, have we not had enough of being cooped up? Hasn't most of our treasure already been spent trying to defend us? Now Zeus is at last granting us the victory, why do you want to depress us into retreating again? I say we set a good watch tonight, sleep soundly and tomorrow arm ourselves early. Even if Achilles returns to the fighting, he can be beaten like any other man."

"The others all agreeing, they then took their supper and slept soundly, while in the Greek camp Achilles led the mourning for Patroclus, swearing that he would not bury his friend until he could bring him the head of Hector and all the

---

[58]

A divine cloak that brings victory to the wearer.

armour he had taken. He swore also to behead twelve Trojan youths at his funeral pyre. At last he gave orders for water to be heated and the body to be washed and anointed with oil, its wounds and gashes filled and sealed with ointments.

Meanwhile Thetis came to the house of Hephaestus where the lame smith-god was working on twenty wheeled tripods. Charis his wife saw her first and greeted her, summoning the god afterwards.

"She is more than welcome," Hephaestus declared, "for she saved me when my own mother Hera wanted to hide me away because I was lame. I owe her my love and many favours."

So he tidied up, put away his tools, wiped his hands, face, chest and neck, put on a fresh tunic and limped to the door with the help of a stick and some wonderfully made devices he had created in the form of living, breathing women. There he greeted his guest and listened to her tale of how Achilles had fallen out with Agamemnon over the priest's daughter Chryseis and so stayed out of the fighting around Troy, with the result that Patroclus now lay dead while Achilles was without armour to avenge him.

The smith-god promptly calmed her grief and returned to his bellows and forge where he first blew up the blaze and began to cast bronze, tin, gold and silver. With these he made a great shield with a shining triple rim and strap of silver, building it up in five layers, on the last of which he engraved scenes of common life. He showed the earth, sky and sea, together with the sun, moon and constellations. He showed two cities. In one, a marriage was being celebrated and a festival taking place as a young man danced and played the flute and lyre. Elsewhere lawsuits were being argued and a public debate held. Around the other city, men fought, led by

Ares and Athene. The besiegers rustled cattle and killed herdsmen while men from the city counter-attacked. Here were Hate, Confusion and Death all casting their spears. But elsewhere the land was being tilled, ploughmen handled their teams and blacked the earth. Here were seen a great chieftain's estates where men reaped corn, carried sheaves and made ready a feast under a tree with a great ox for sacrifice. Vines heavy with grapes twined themselves around silver poles, and girls and young men carried baskets of the fruit away while a young man with a lyre sang the beautiful harvest song of Linus.[59] The smith-god also showed a lovely valley with flocks and cottages scattered about and a dancing floor like the one Daedalus built for Ariadne at Cnossus, the girls all in floating dresses with garlands, the young men in glowing tunics with golden knives on belts of silver. There were acrobats too.

All round the great shield ran the river of Ocean, and when it was finished, the smith-god made chest armour brighter even than his fire, together with a huge and intricate helmet and leg-armour.[60] When all was ready, he laid it at the feet of the mother of Achilles who swept down to earth with it like a hawk from the snows of Olympus.

---

[59]

A mysterious mythical subject - the Linus Song (but possibly even a person) - known all over the eastern Mediterranean and perhaps to do with the harvest and changing of the seasons.

[60]

Perhaps the most famous passage in the epic, this shield of Achilles evokes the whole ancient everyday Greek world of which war was an inevitable part - but only a part.

Book 19

Now saffron-robed Dawn arose from her ocean bed and Thetis came to the Greek ships where Achilles still wept, his arms round the dead Patroclus and his companions around him.

"Son," she said, "it is time to leave grieving and put on the armour Hephaestus has made for you."

Achilles' companions were too afraid to inspect its unearthly beauty, but Achilles did, and as he did, his grief turned to a terrible anger.

"Mother, I want to do as you suggest, but the son of Menoetius's body will rot and stink if I leave it here for long."

"Son, I will take care of that. If you were away a year, you would still come back to find it firmer and more fragrant than now."

With that she inspired him with huge courage and dripped ambrosia and red nectar into the dead man's nostrils, after which Achilles stalked along the sea-shore, uttering his terrible cry and summoning to council all the Greeks – even the artisans who looked after the ships and those who kept the fighting men supplied. The injured chiefs, including Agamemnon who was still pained by the wound given him by the son of Antenor's spear, attended as well.

"Son of Atreus, greatest of men, "Achilles announced when they were assembled, "how I wish Artemis had killed the girl we argued over that day I destroyed her city and captured her, for that would have been better for both Greeks and Trojans. Still, let us end our squabbling now and find out whether the Trojans are brave enough to sleep beside our ships tonight."

Agamemnon spoke up. "Achilles, and all you other Greeks, do not hold me at fault for ever for my madness that day when I stripped Achilles of his prize. Zeus, Destiny and the Furies were to blame. Delusion,[61] Zeus's eldest daughter, deceived even her own father when he swore an oath that Heracles, his son about to be born by Theban Alcmene, would be greatest of men, only for Hera to trick him by slowing Alcmene's contractions and inducing the birth of Eristheus of Argos first. When he realized what she had done, Zeus caught his daughter by the hair and flung her out of the sky but could still only grieve thereafter as Heracles had to perform all the labours Eristheus imposed on him. I too was deluded – or Zeus stole my wits. But now I make over to Achilles all that I promised and Odysseus offered him before."

"Son of Atreus, lordliest of men,"[62] Achilles answered, "give or keep your gifts, as you see fit. Now, though, it is better that we go to work at once on the [63]Trojans."

---

[61] Homer's gods are a very mixed crowd. Among Olympians and survivors of older religions, they number others who embody natural forces - or simply, as here, personify abstract notions.

[62] Note how formally and courteously Achilles and Agamemnon now behave towards each other. Civility's most important job has always been to contain savagery.

"Not before we have eaten," Odysseus interrupted[63]. However much men may want to fight, they cannot do so on empty bellies. So let them ready themselves with a good meal while Agamemnon's servants bring out his gifts for all to look at and admire. Then let him swear an oath that he has not touch Briseis, the girl he took from you to replace Chryseis. Finally, let him feast you ceremoniously as is right and proper."

"Well said," answered Agamemnon. "You yourself, Odysseus, choose the best of the young men to help you fetch the gifts from my quarters while the herald Talthybius prepares a boar pig for Zeus's sacrifice."

"Great Agamemnon," Achilles objected stubbornly, "no man should eat while he lives with shame. Let us fight first, then cleanse ourselves. We can feast when day is over."

But Odysseus stood his ground. "No, Achilles, you are stronger than me and the better fighter, but I make more sense than you. Starving is a bad way to mourn. Harden your heart, eat well — then make your enemies sorry for your strength."

He then left with Nestor's two fine sons, Meges, Meriones, Thoas, Lycomedes and Melanippus to fetch Agamemnon's gifts, including the girl Briseis, and weighed out ten talents of gold while back at the assembly Agamemnon prayed and swore a great oath that he had not touched the girl while she had been with him and slit the boar's throat, after which Talthybius the herald threw its carcase into the surf for the

---

[63]

Typically, it is Odysseus, who reminds them that an army marches on its stomach and is also enough to want this dispute settled finally and in public.

fishes to eat. Now all the Greeks scattered to feed while Achilles' Myrmidons took the gifts to his quarters. Arriving there, beautiful Briseis wept to see Patroclus's body laid out.

"Patroclus, when Achilles sacked my city and killed my parents and brothers, it was you who looked after me and promised to make me Achilles' wife. You were always kind to me."[64]

The other Greek chieftains then begged Achilles to eat, but he still refused, preferring to lament. "There is no death worse I could be made to suffer than yours, Patroclus," he groaned, "not even my old father's or my son's whom I left behind at home. Before this, I had hoped to be the first to die far from home so that you at least could take my son from Scyros and show him his father's possessions."

Filled with pity, Zeus then encouraged Athene to distil strength-giving nectar and ambrosia into him while the others filled their bellies so that afterwards the earth laughed beneath them as they all went to battle. Achilles put on the immortal armour made for him by Hephaestus and took from its case Peleus's great ash spear which only he could wield. Then he climbed into his chariot and spoke to his horses, immortal foals of Podarge, rebuking them for not having brought their master home the last time they were in harness.

One of them, Xanthus, answered him: "We can keep you safe this time, Achilles," the great horse said, "but after that you yourself must die, felled by a god and a mortal."

---

[64] Compare this passage with the later lament of Helen over the body of Hector (Book 24). In both, the dead are feelingly lamented by women, the biggest losers in all conflicts - even those on the other 'side'.

Book 20

Now while the great armies deployed, Zeus sent Themis to summon the gods to assembly. Every river except Ocean[65] and every nymph of wood, spring and field was there. Poseidon also attended and asked his great brother if the resumption of fighting was the cause of their assembly.

"It is," Zeus answered. "I myself will just sit and watch the battle, but all you other gods may now join in on whichever side you fancy, for without interference from we immortals, Achilles is likely to storm Ilium in spite of fate."

So the gods descended to earth and the fighting: Hera, Athene, Poseidon, Hermes and Hephaestus siding with the Greeks; Ares, Apollo, Artemis, Aphrodite, Leto and Xanthus with the Trojans. At first the Trojans retreated, but then the immortals fired their passion to resist while Zeus thundered from above and Poseidon so rocked all the land with quakes

---

[65] Of course Olympian society was like Greek society, so they called councils on important occasions. Ocean was thought of as a great waterway circling all solid earth while every spot and feature of earth and sea had its presiding nymph, or genius. The fact that all are called to attend underlines the decisiveness of this moment in history.

that Aedoneus[66], lord of the Underworld below, screamed in terror.

Then Achilles raged all over the battlefield searching for Hector, but Apollo, momentarily taking the shape of Priam's son Lycaon, urged Aeneas to fight him instead. Pointing out that he, too, was a goddess's son, he filled him with enormous strength. So Aeneas advanced on Achilles — at which Hera, concerned for the outcome, consulted with the other gods. Knowing that Aeneas was not destined to be killed at Troy, while Achilles was, Poseidon urged restraint and suggested that they interfere only if Apollo or any of the other gods on the Trojan side did. This being agreed, they all then withdrew from the fighting, the Greek-supporters to the stronghold built long since to help Heracles avoid the charging sea beast,[67] Trojan-supporters to hills on the other side.

As the warriors closed, Achilles asked Aeneas what he hoped to gain by fighting him, mocking him about the last time they met. "That time I chased you all the way to Lyrenessus,"[68] he reminded him. "Only the gods saved you then."

"Achilles," answered Aeneas, "you and I do not need words to frighten each other, but if you want to know more about who you are fighting, know that immortal Zeus had a son

---

66

Another name for the Hades, the Underworld god, presumably not called to the council since death is universal and all, except the immortals, being subject to it.

67

Sent by Poseidon against Troy in an earlier myth and killed by Heracles.

68

A town in the Troad where Achilles' Briseis came from.

Dardanus who in turn fathered a son, Ericthonius, richest of men of his day and owner of three thousand horses. Ericthonius in turn fathered Tros, to whom were born Ilus, Assaracus and Ganymede. Ilus then also had sons, who included Priam, while Assaracus fathered my father, Anchises. But that is enough. Words are but tricky and childish things, better suited to squabbling women than to fighting men. Now let us test each other's strength."

"With that, he drove his spear hard at Achilles' shield but could not pierce the war god's own workmanship. In reply, Achilles threw so hard that his spear tore through the rim of Aeneas's shield where the bronze was thinnest, thudding into the ground beyond as the other ducked to avoid it. Then he drew his sword and rushed at Aeneas, who grabbed and threw a boulder heavier than any two men could lift today. But Achilles would have fended off that and killed Aeneas with his sword had not Poseidon intervened.

"Aeneas will die if we do not save him," he told the other gods, "before his time and despite the sacrifices he has made to us over the years. Zeus will be angry as well, for Aeneas is fated to survive this war, save the house of his favourite son Dardanus and one day rule in Troy himself."[69]

When the others would do nothing in spite of this urging, he himself made his way through the battle, arriving just in time. Cloaking both combatants in a deep mist, he retrieved Achilles' spear, dropping it at its owner's feet, while lifting

---

[69]

Some 700 years on the Roman poet Virgil will fashion a new Latin epic out of this passage, changing only one detail: that Aeneas will found the Roman empire rather than rule in Troy (but for Virgil, Rome *was* the new Troy)!

Aeneas like a child and tossing him bodily to the fringes of the fighting where he himself then confronted him.

"Aeneas, if Apollo tries again to get you to fight Achilles, refuse or die, for Achilles is dearer to the gods than you are. Once he is dead, though, you may fight again in the front rank, for no other Greek will be able to kill you."

Meanwhile Achilles rubbed the mist from his eyes, saw his own spear lying on the ground at his feet and Aeneas gone. Concluding rightly that the man was god-protected, he shrugged, urged his men on and himself turned to find battle elsewhere. First he killed Iphition, whose body was promptly cut to pieces by chariot wheel rims, then Demoleon, Hippodamas, and Priam's son Polydorus who died holding his spilt bowels in his hands, having taken Achilles' spear in the small of his back. Now Hector was infuriated by a brother's death and looked for vengeance, but Athene puffed his spear-cast aside while Apollo caught him up in a mist and whirled him away. Three times Achilles stabbed into the impenetrable murk before again giving up and looking for other targets.

Now he hit Dryops in the neck with the spear, then he killed huge Demolion, the brothers Dardanus and Leogonus, Alastor's son Tros who died even as he begged for his life, then Mulius, Echeclus and Deucalion. He killed Thracian Rhigmus as well together with Areithous his co-charioteer. Like a mountain fire lashed by the wind or the huge oxen crushing barley on a threshing floor, he raged everywhere, his horses trampling dead men whose blood splashed up on his chariot's underside and wheels.

Book 21

When he came to Xanthus, the river that was a son of Zeus, Achilles split the Trojans into two groups, chasing the one across the open plain towards the city, the other into a loop of the river where, armed only with his sword, he leapt in and killed many. Among them was Lycaon, one of Priam's sons whom he had already captured once before and sold into slavery on Lemnos. The man had since been bought by friends and been back only twelve days among his own people.

"Spare me, Achilles!" Lycaon screamed. "I am the unluckiest man still alive. Remember, I was not born to the same mother as Hector, even though we share a father, and you will get good ransom for me."

"Fool," retorted Achilles. "Why so much fuss over dying? Patroclus, who was a better man than you, lies dead and some day soon an arrow or a spear will take my life as well."

Then, as the other seized his knees to plead further, he buried his sword to the hilt in the angle of the man's neck before grabbing the body by a foot and heaving it into the river.

"Now let the fishes can have you – and so die all Trojans to pay for the death of Patroclus and those Greeks who were killed while I stayed out of the fighting."

Now the river grew angry and sent against him Asteropaeus, a man himself born of a river who managed to wound him in the arm, but Achilles killed him as well along with so many others that the river god had to beg him to stop before his channels became clogged, but Achilles raged on until, finally, the river god himself rose against him as a wall of water threatening to drown or chase him across the plain. Then Athene and Poseidon had to comfort their champion, but now Xanthus called on his brother river Simoïs for help, so Hera sent Hephaestus to fight water with fire. Hephaestus then singed all the plain with his heat and boiled Xanthus's waters while Hera sent strong, withering west and south winds, singeing the elms, willows and tamarisks along his banks. Now even fish and eels leapt from his scalding waters until he persuaded Hera and Poseidon to relent.

Zeus alone on Olympus laughed to see the other gods fighting. Now Ares attacked Athene — who laid him out with a huge stone. Aphrodite had to help the stricken war god away but was attacked in her turn as Hera urged Athene to fetch her a great thump to the breasts that sent the love-goddess sprawling.

"Well," sighed Poseidon to Apollo, "I suppose we two will have to join in, so since you are my junior, you can strike me first.[70] But you are a fool to champion these Trojans. Have you forgotten what Laomedon put us through after I built a wall for the Trojans' city while you herded their cattle on the slopes of Ida? He refused to pay us for our labour then and even threatened to make slaves of us."

---

[70] Now the war has become literally universal. Homer shows that even nature depends on the harmony and proper functioning of its component elements - and that war can disrupt them. Note too, though, that Shakespeare did not invent the mixing of comedy with tragedy!

"I would be mad to fight my own uncle," the younger god answered him civilly," especially for the sake of mere mortals who are like leaves that flutter and turn in the sunlight, only to fall soon after. Let them fight their own battles."

Hearing him, his sister Artemis, the lady of wild animals, interrupted bitterly. "You wriggle out of fighting your uncle, do you? You who always boasted you could beat him."

Apollo did not answer, but Hera, angry at her, grabbed the hunter-goddess's wrists with one hand while clouting her about the head with her own bow and quiver with the other. Weeping, the younger goddess ran to her father Zeus who laughed, cuddled and comforted her.

But when all the other gods had turned their backs on the fighting and returned to Olympus, Apollo alone returned to Troy, afraid that Achilles might yet storm its walls in spite of fate. By then Priam had ordered the gates to be opened so that his fleeing Trojans could reach shelter inside. In case the raging Achilles should accidentally be let in as well, though, Apollo sent brilliant Agenor, Antenor's son, against him. This man knew he had little chance but nevertheless chose bravery, confronting Achilles and even scoring a hard hit on a greave with his spear. Then Achilles leapt at him, enraged, but Apollo shrouded the man in a mist and used him to lead the Greek on a pointless chase all over the battlefield. Thus all the other Trojans were able to escape within the gates, which were then shut fast.

Book 22

When all were safe inside, Phoebus Apollo stopped leading Achilles astray, appeared to him openly and mocked him for chasing an immortal.

"If you were less than a god, you would pay for your tricks," Achilles retorted angrily, turning back immediately to race back to Troy like that brightest of stars, Orion's Dog, that brings mankind such grief in the Autumn.[71] Priam saw him first and implored his son to retreat within city walls. His mother bared her breasts to move him to pity, but Hector stayed outside to confront Achilles, knowing that if he had listened to Polydamas his people would not now be in the situation they were in.

"I trusted in my strength before," he reflected calmly, "and must do so now. It is too late to hope to make peace."

So he waited bravely until Achilles actually appeared, but then suddenly panicked and ran. Peleus's son followed, and so they raced for more than the usual prize. Zeus himself looked down in pity on Hector, for as in a nightmare, the pursued man was unable outrun his pursuer while the pursuer himself could not catch up. Athene put an end to their stalemate. Stopping

---

[71]

Alpha canis majora, the dog-star, its bright rising in July-September is associated with hot and humid conditions and, therefore, of discomfort and illness as well. Note now the more elegiac tone as Hector's death approaches.

by Achilles, she told him to rest and catch his breath while she persuaded Hector to fight. Then she stopped by Hector in the guise of Deïphobus, promising him help. Heartened by the illusion that at least one of his brothers would second him, Hector then stood his ground and tried to persuade Achilles that whoever survived their encounter should at least give the other's body back for burial. Achilles, though, would listen to no deal.

"No agreements, Hector. I can never forgive you."

Then he threw his spear, which Hector ducked. He did not see Athene catch and return it to the other's hand. Meanwhile his own spear rebounded from the centre of Achilles' shield, but when he called to Deïphobus for another and got no answer, he realized the trick that had been played on him.[72]

"So be it," he told himself. "Death stares at me, but let it not be without a glorious struggle."

So he drew his great sword and charged, but Achilles watched, noted the unprotected spot at the base of the throat in his own armour - and lunged. His windpipe still unsevered, Hector could still, just, speak.

"Give my body back for burial," he pleaded.

"Never," answered Achilles. "Not if Priam himself offered me your weight in gold. The dogs and birds can have you."

---

[72]

While Apollo had a hand in the killing of Patroclus, Athene for once has to help Achilles. Perhaps it is the greatness of heroes that the gods' help is always apparent in what they do.

"I knew I would not persuade you — but Paris and Apollo will avenge me."[73]

So Hector's spirit fluttered free and went down to death's house, mourning youth and manhood left behind. Achilles pulled his spear free and stripped the body of his own armour while the other Greeks ran up, wondered and stabbed at it with their spears.

"We will see what the Trojans do now," Achilles said, "But first we will bury Patroclus whom I will remember even when I, too, am dead."

His heart full of pain and grief, he pierced Hector's heels behind the tendons, threaded ox-hide straps through, fastened the ends to his chariot and whipped up his horses. When he saw what was being done to his son, Priam had to be restrained in his grief while Hecuba led the women's wailing, and it was this that forewarned Andromache as she sat spinning in her house, ignorant of what had happened. Now fearing the worst, she ran with her women to the city wall, saw her husband's body and fainted clean away. Coming to, she threw off her diadem and headdress that golden Aphrodite had given her when she married and herself led the mourning.

"Hector, how I wish I had never been born now that you are dead, leaving your son fatherless. Even if he survives the Greeks, he can look forward only to a life without kindness, for although some may spare him a sip or a crust out of pity, most will shove him away, unprotected as he is. Now, Hector, you

---

[73] At the gate of death, Homer's heroes often prophecy. Hector here foretells Achilles' death by an arrow shot by Paris into his heel - his Achilles heel.

yourself will be naked food for dogs while I must burn those beautiful clothes you will never wear again."

So she mourned in tears and the women of Troy with her.

Book 23

Now while the rest of the Greeks dispersed to their ships, Achilles and his Myrmidons still mourned Patroclus, riding their horses three times round his bier, weeping and wailing continually until, after throwing Hector's body face-down beside the bier as a further insult, Achilles feasted them all on oxen, sheep, goats and pigs. Now the other chieftains and Agamemnon, who had set a great cauldron over a fire, tried to persuade him to wash the blood and battle filth from his body, but he refused.

"Before Zeus, best and greatest of gods, I have sworn not to let water touch my head until I have buried Patroclus and cut my hair off for him. For the moment, let us eat and tomorrow fetch wood for his pyre."

So they all did as he asked and afterwards dispersed to their quarters. Achilles, though, rested restlessly on the beach by the sounding sea — where Patroclus's ghost now appeared to him.

"Have you forgotten me so quickly?" it groaned. "Burn and bury me, Achilles, so that I can pass through Hades' gates, even though afterwards we two will never see each other again. Ever since Menoetius brought me, an accidental killer,[74] to your

---

[74] See the note at the end on Patroclus's story. According to ancient belief, a body could not be ferried across the River Styx into the Underworld until properly buried.

father's house when I was a boy, you and I have never been separated, so let us be inseparable in death. Let one golden urn hold both our ashes."

The sleeping Achilles agreed and woke after trying in vain to embrace his dead friend whose spirit had vanished again like smoke. Then he told the Myrmidons his dream, and at dawn Agamemnon sent Meriones and the other young men out timber-gathering. Venturing onto Ida's shaggy slopes, they cut and split oaks which they dragged to Achilles' appointed place, and there the Myrmidons brought Patroclus's body, built a pyre, and Achilles cut off the lock of his own hair which he had promised Spercheus[75] even though the other had not granted his prayer for a safe return.

Then they all dispersed except for the assembled Greek chiefs and the Myrmidons who now sacrificed cattle, horses, jars of oil and honey and two of Patroclus's nine hounds. There, too, Achilles cut the throats of twelve young well-born Trojans, laying their bodies around the pyre's edge - but not the body of Hector himself which he had sworn to feed to dogs.[76] Aphrodite herself, though, was careful to fend away any damage from it, anointing its head with immortal oil while Phoebus Apollo himself kept off the sun's harsh rays.

At first the pyre refused to light, but Achilles prayed to Boreas and Zephyrus, north and west winds, and Iris carried

---

[75]

A river in the region of Thessaly (central Greece) that was Achilles' home.

[76]

A barbaric send-off that contrasts with the courtliness shown in the funeral games that follow. The use of honey and oil may recall a time when bodies were embalmed.

his prayer to where these were feasting. They came immediately, roaring down on the Troad, and soon the pyre blazed fiercely. All that night it burned while Achilles poured wine round it and called on the spirit of the dead man. In the morning he slept beside the ashes until they had cooled and once again the Greek chiefs appeared, this time to gather up Patroclus's bones from the pyre's centre and seal them in a golden jar which they placed in a modest grave until Achilles himself should also die and his bones be added to those of his friend.

Now Achilles made the whole army sit in assembly while his men brought out treasure from his storerooms as prizes to be competed for in memorial games in honour of the dead man: cauldrons, horses, mules, cattle, iron, women.[77] For the chariot race first prize, he set out a skilled serving woman and an eared tripod; for the second prize, a six-year old unbroken mare in foal; for third, an unfired cauldron; for fourth, two talents of gold; for fifth, an unfired jar with two handles. Then he called for contenders, exempting his own divine team.

Eumelus, Diomedes, Nestor's son Antilochus — to whom his father gave long and detailed advice and instructions — Menelaus and Meriones all climbed up into their chariots, and when Phoenix had been stationed at the halfway turning mark to act as umpire, the race was started. Soon the chariots were

---

[77]

Ceremonial games were held at Olympia from at least Homer's onwards and directly inspired our Olympic Games. The choice of prizes gives an idea of relative values in the ancient Greek world - and note that while Achilles will cause mayhem rather than have a woman taken from him, he will graciously give one away as a prize!

strung out across the plain, Eumelus in the lead but with Diomedes' horses breathing down his neck. Diomedes might even have caught him, but Apollo knocked the whip from his hand - at which Athene picked it up and restored it to him, while also causing Eumelus's chariot to crash so that now Diomedes led with, just behind him, Antilochus who was lashing on his father's horses.

"Come on you two"' Antilochus bellowed. "You may not be as good as Diomedes' nags, but you can match Menelaus's!"

In fact he drew level in a narrow, dangerous place, alarming Menelaus so much that the older man shouted a warning for him to keep back. Antilochus ignored him, though, and whipped on his team the harder - with the result that Menelaus had to drop back and let him pass. He was not pleased.

Back at the assembly, it was Idomeneus who first spotted Diomedes' team in the lead, one of the latter's horses being a distinctive red roan with a white blaze. He announced the fact excitedly, thereby annoying Oïlean Ajax who thought Eumelus was in front, and the two exchanged hard words until pacified by Achilles. Diomedes romped home to settle the issue anyway, followed by Antilochus and Menelaus who just failed to make up the ground he had been forced to lose. Meriones was well down the field. Even further back was Eumelus, dragging his chariot and driving his horses ahead of him.

Pitying Eumelus, Achilles asked the assembly to agree with him in awarding him the second prize since he was actually the best of the contestants. Antilochus, though, took exception to this, urging him to give Eumelus some other prize and warning that he would fight to keep what he had won.

Achilles, who liked the younger man, smiled.[78] "Very well, Antilochus, for your sake I will give Eumelus the armour I took from Asteropaeus, and you can keep the mare in foal."

But now Menelaus spoke up. "But that prize is rightfully mine," he growled, "not Antilochus's. He baulked and cheated me — let him deny it if he can."

Antilochus immediately offered him the mare. "Menelaus, you know how inconsiderate and stupid young men are. You are the older and wiser and of course you are in the right. If there is anything else you want of mine, tell me and you shall have that as well."

Menelaus immediately relented. "Now it is my turn to give way. You were always a fine boy, Antilochus, and you and your father and brother have done a lot for the Greeks. Take your prize back, even though she was rightfully mine.'

So Menelaus accepted the cauldron instead and Meriones the two talents of gold. That, though, still left the fifth prize, which Achilles presented to Nestor in tribute to his age and ancient prowess, prompting the old man to tell them the story of how, at funeral games held at Buprasion years before, he won the boxing against Clyptomedes, the wrestling against Ancaeus, the sprinting against Iphicus and javelin against Polydorus and Phyleus.

"May the gods grant you happiness, Achilles," he finished, "for so honouring me today."

---

[78]

Apart from introducing a dramatic shift in mood and tone, Achilles' games show how passions like pride and ambition that drive the fighter are inseparable from, under gentler circumstances, courtesy, magnanimity, and generosity of the sportsman (and gentleman).

Now Achilles set out prizes for the boxing: a hard-working she-ass for the winner; for the loser a two-handled goblet. Epeius was first to step out, cheerfully warning the friends of anyone rash enough to stand up to him to remember their first-aid skills since he intended to beat their man to a pulp. The experienced Euryalus took him on – but almost immediately took a punch to the cheekbone that would have laid him out cold had Epeius himself not grabbed and held him upright. The man was still groggy and spitting blood when his seconds went to collect his loser's prize.

Next Achilles set out prizes for the wrestling: a great tripod for the winner, valued at twelve oxen; for the loser a skilled servant woman. To contest them, huge Telamonian Ajax and wily Odysseus stripped off and faced each other, but neither could win a decisive fall for all their heaving, so Achilles finally stopped the contest and declared them joint winners.

For the foot-race, he set out a great silver mixing-bowl of Phoenician workmanship that had once belonged to Patroclus; for second place there was a great ox; for the third a half-talent of gold. In this contest Odysseus again stood up, this time against Oïlean Ajax and Antilochus. The swift Ajax led the field for most of the distance, followed by Odysseus almost in his footsteps. On the last stretch, though, Odysseus made a prayer to Athene who helped him overhaul the other — who in any case slipped and fell in an ox-pat left over from the funeral sacrifice, staggering home with his face plastered with the stuff, to everyone huge amusement.

"As they always do, the gods favour old men," Antilochus grumbled as he came in. "No-one ever could catch Odysseus — except Achilles, of course."

Pleased by the compliment, Achilles added another half-talent to the young man's third prize before setting out the magnificent spear, shield and helmet that had once been the arms of Sarpedon.

"Now for a real fight. I want two men. The first to get in a telling spear-thrust against the other and draw blood will receive this silver-nailed Thracian sword and belt that I took off Asteropaeus. Both contestants, though, will share the arms of Sarpedon — and a dinner in my tent."

Armoured and menacing, Telamonian Ajax and Diomedes now faced up to each other. Ajax stabbed at Diomedes' shield but could not penetrate it, so that afterwards his own neck was continually threatened by Diomedes' spear over the rim of his shield. Concerned, the other Greeks cried out for the contest to be stopped and the prizes shared. So Achilles obliged, but awarded Asteropaeus's great sword and belt to Diomedes.

Now he put out a great lump of pig-iron, enough to keep a winner's estate in tools for five years, as the shot-putting prize. Polypoites, Leonteus, Telamonian Ajax and Epeius all tried their hands. Ajax overthrew all those before him, but Polypoites threw last - and overthrew everyone else.

Next, Achilles set out more iron in the form of ten double-bladed axes and ten single ones. Tethering a pigeon by one leg to a ship's mast set up on land, he promised the double-axes to anyone who could kill the bird - or, failing that, the single axes to anyone who could sever the cord securing it. Teucer and Meriones took up the challenge and drew lots. Teucer won and so shot first - but failed to pray to the archer-god Apollo who caused him to cut the cord only, releasing the pigeon which quickly made for the clouds. Just as quickly though, but not too quickly to pray first, Meriones then shot, and his arrow went clean through the bird, the arrow falling at his feet while the bird fell by the mast. Thus he carried off the double-axes.

For spear-throwing, Achilles set out a spear and a patterned unfired cauldron. Agamemnon and Meriones stood up – but Achilles then cancelled the contest. "Great Agamemnon, we already know you are the Greeks' greatest spear-thrower," he said, "so take the cauldron — and I suggest you award the spear to Meriones."

Pleased, Agamemnon did as he suggested, handing his own magnificent prize to his herald Talthybius.

Book 24

When the games were over, the army went back to its quarters to eat and sleep. Only Achilles still grieved, unable either to sleep or to forget Patroclus. Every morning he dragged the body of Hector round the barrow to insult it further although Apollo still kept it from damage and corruption. Finally, even the gods condemned the nine-day outrage, some urging Hermes to steal the corpse. Zeus, though, ordered Iris to fetch Thetis, so Thetis came out of the depths of the sea and was told to go to her son and tell him that Olympus was angry, that he was to return Hector's body to the Trojans in exchange for gifts.

Now too he sent Iris to Priam to load a wagon with gifts and, guarded by Hermes, drive it to the Greek ships to beg back the body of his son. So Iris came down to Troy and found the old man shrouded in a cloak, huddled and weeping in his courtyard, covered with animal dung which he had thrown over himself. She gave him Zeus's message, whereupon he told his wife and ordered his sons to make a wagon ready. Then he went up to his storerooms and gathered treasure: twelve mantles and the same number of blankets, cloaks and tunics together with ten talents of gold, two tripods, four cauldrons and a beautifully chased goblet of Thracian workmanship.

Grabbing a stick, he chased the bystanders from his corridors of his palace, ordered his nine surviving sons to finish making his wagon ready and then load it with the ransom he had gathered. Hecuba appeared before he left to urge a drink-offering to Zeus and beg for a bird of omen as reassurance. So Priam did as she asked, and at once Zeus sent a great black eagle on the right hand, seeing which the old man mounted his wagon with his old driver Idaeus and left the city.

Soon they came to flat land where those who had followed them turned back, so Zeus sent the god Hermes to Priam in the shape of noble, fresh-bearded youth. As the wagon passed the tomb of Ilus, the travellers saw the god approach and were afraid, but Hermes calmed and reassured them that the old man's dead son still lay undecayed and unmarred beside Achilles' ships. Refusing a gift, he himself then jumped up to take the reins and drove the wagon to the fortifications, causing the sentries' heads to nod as he opened the massive gates to Achilles' headquarters and unloaded the old man's gifts. Then Priam entered the building alone, leaving Idaeus outside to guard the horses and mules.

He found Achilles with two other men, approached him unseen and seized and kissed the huge, deadly hands that had killed so many of his sons.

"Achilles, call to mind your own father who must be the same age as me, even though he at least can still hope to see his son come home again. I am not so lucky. I had fifty sons until the Greeks came, nineteen of them out of the one mother. Now most are dead in battle while the greatest of them all, the guardian of our city, was killed a few days ago. I bring you great gifts to buy his body back. Have pity on me, Achilles. No man has ever been forced to do what I now do — put my lips to the hands of the man who killed my sons."

The younger gently pushed the older man's hand away, and together they wept, Priam for Hector, Achilles for his old father and the dead Patroclus. When they were finished, the younger raised the older up.

"How did you dare come here alone through so many enemies to confront the man who has killed so many of your sons? Your spirit must be iron, but it is Zeus's way that men must live in unhappiness, finding at least as many sorrows as blessings in their lives. My father was the luckiest man alive, blessed even with a goddess for a wife, yet now he is old, weak and alone while I am far away bringing nothing but misery to you here who, they say, once owned enormous wealth and lands. Well, there is point in grieving over what cannot be changed."

"Beloved of Zeus," Priam replied, "do not keep me waiting. Accept my ransom. Give me back my son."

There was menace in Achilles' answer. "Old man, do not press this. I myself already have chosen to give your son's body back. Do not make me turn on you."

Frightened, Priam huddled quietly while Achilles leapt powerfully to the door to summon Automedon and Alcimus, the men closest to him since the death of Patroclus. These two brought Idaeus inside and fetched Priam's gifts while servant women washed and anointed Hector's corpse out of Priam's sight for fear that neither the old man nor he would not be able to restrain their grief and anger. When all was ready, Achilles himself lifted and carried the body to the wagon, calling on Patroclus's spirit as he did so.

"Forgive me, Patroclus. The ransom I got was a good one — and you will have your share."

"You will see your son when you return to Troy at dawn," he told Priam, "but now we will eat. Even Niobe, after all her children had been killed by Apollo and Artemis, had to leave off grieving and eat eventually."[79]

Again he bounded up, this time to kill a sheep which his companions then butchered and roasted expertly. When they had eaten, they relaxed enough to inspect each other. Both of them marvelled at what they saw, but finally Priam begged Achilles for a bed, telling him he had just eaten and now needed sleep for the first time since his son died. So Achilles ordered his serving men and women to make up the beds in the porch and questioned him on how long he needed to bury Hector so that the Greeks could be held back from attack during that time.

"My people are penned in and afraid," Priam answered, "and will need to cut and fetch wood from the hills. We will mourn him nine days in my palace and burn him on the tenth. On the eleventh we will build him a grave-barrow and on the twelfth fight again if we must."

So Achilles agreed to hold off that period of time and sent him and Idaeus to their beds in the porch while he himself went to sleep beside the beautiful Briseis. And so all rested until Hermes woke Priam in the dark to remind him that if other Greeks found him before he returned to his city, it would be dangerous. So Priam wakened Idaeus while Hermes harnessed the mules and horses and himself conducted them

---

[79]
In the best-known of all Greek myths of sorrow, Niobe boasted of her many children to the goddess Leto who had only two: Apollo and Artemis. She promptly killed those of Niobe - who then wept until turned to a column of weeping stone.

through the camp again undetected. The god left them at the ford across Xanthus river.

Beautiful Cassandra was the first to see her father approaching from the height of Pergamos, Troy's citadel. She roused the city so that all came out to meet and mourn the dead Hector, making it hard for Priam to reach his palace. Andromache was first to lament, cradling her husband's head in her arms.

"Husband, you have left behind a child who will not grow old since he no longer has a father to protect him. He and I will be sent into slavery, or killed by some Greek who is bitter over what you did to his brother or son or father.[80] I, though, will mourn you most since we never had chance to exchange last words in life."

Then Hecuba lamented.

"Dearest to me of all my sons, as you were to the gods who have looked after you even in death. Now you can sleep in your palace fresh and beautiful as ever for all the harm Achilles tried to do your body."

Third and last, Helen led the song of sorrow.

"Hector, I loved you best of all your brothers. I wish I had died before Paris brought me here twenty years ago, yet in all those years, from you alone I never heard a harsh word while you restrained others who would have been unkind to me. Therefore I mourn for myself as well as for you. No-one else was ever so kind and gentle to me."

---

[80]

A prophetic foretelling of what was actually to happen as described in Euripides' play *Trojan Women*.

Finally Priam gave orders for the collecting of timber, promising his people that they would be free from attack until the twelfth day. So they harnessed their mules and made preparations, and on the tenth day they burned Hector's body. On the dawn of the eleventh, they put out the pyre with wine, collected the bones in a golden casket which they wrapped in purple, buried it in a tomb covered with massive stone slabs and piled high over it a barrow. Afterwards they held a great feast in the house of Priam, their king under Zeus.

Such was the burial of Hector, tamer of horses.

Gods, heroes and others

Achilles: Chief Greek hero the *Iliad* and leader of the Myrmidons. According to legend he was made almost invulnerable by being dipped in the Underworld river of Styx, only his (Achilles) heel, by which he was held, remaining unprotected..

Aeneas: Son of Aphrodite and Anchises. A leading Trojan chief who survived the fall of Troy and (according to Virgil) migrated to Italy and become the hero the *Aeneid*.

Agamemnon: Joint leader with his younger brother Menelaus of the Greeks. Murdered on his return by his wife Clytemnaestra and her lover Aegisthus.

Agenor: A Trojan chief, son of Antenor.

Ajax: Either of: huge Telamonian Ajax or the lesser Locrian Ajax, a son of Oïleus.

Andromache: Wife of Hector and mother of Astyanax.

Antenor: An important Trojan elder with little sympathy for Helen since he lost many sons in the war.

Antilochus: A son of Nestor and one of the most prominent younger Greek chiefs.

Aphrodite: Goddess of love, daughter of Zeus, a supporter of the Trojans.

Apollo: Son of Zeus and an archer-god. Also called Phoebus ('the Bright') or Phoebus Apollo. Associated with prophecy, music and plagues.

Ares: God of war, son of Zeus and Hera and a Trojan supporter.

Argos: A place name, sometimes denoting the city of Diomedes, sometimes that of Achilles - sometimes meaning just 'Greece'.

Ariadne: A daughter of Minos who fell in love with the legendary hero Theseus and helped him kill the sacred bull of Minos and escape from Crete.

Artemis: Goddess daughter of Zeus and sister of Apollo. Huntress, archer and another killer by disease, though of women only.

Asclepius: Son of Apollo, god of medicine, who learned his trade under the wise centaur Chiron. Killed by Zeus for restoring Hippolytus to life.

Astyanax: Also known as Scamandrius, son of Hector and Andromache.

Athene: (Also called Pallas Athene) A daughter of Zeus who fights on the Greek side. Associated with wisdom, women in childbirth and the arts and crafts.

Automedon: Achilles' and Patroclus's charioteer.

Bellerophon: A mythical Greek hero who tamed the winged horse Pegasus, killed the monster Chimaera and defeated the Amazons.

Briseis: A Trojan girl, Achilles' prize, whom he had gave up to compensate Agamemnon for the latter's loss of Chryseis — the cause of the *Iliad*'s great quarrel.

Calchas: Chief Greek seer who accompanied the Greeks to Troy.

Cassandra: Daughter of Priam and a prophetess fated never to be believed (because she bargained her virginity to the god Apollo in exchange for the gift of prophecy but then reneged on the deal).

Chimaera: a Lycian monster usually depicted with a lion's head, goat's body and serpent's tail.

Chryseis: Daughter of Chryses, the Trojan priest of Apollo, whom Agamemnon restored to her father to save the Greek army from disease.

Cronos: Once the supreme god, husband of Rhea and father of Zeus, Poseidon and Hades. Deposed and castrated by Zeus.

Daedalus: A legendary Athenian craftsman who built the famous labyrinth to contain the bull of Minos on the island of Crete from which he himself had to escape with his son Icarus.

Demeter: Sister of Zeus and goddess of corn and agriculture.

Deïphobus: Another of Priam's sons and one of the Trojans' stronger fighters.

Diomedes: One of the major Greek heroes.

Dione: Aphrodite's mother. A shadowy goddess whose name may simply be the feminine of Zeus.

Eos: Goddess of the dawn and mother of the hero Memnon by Tithonus, for whose death she was said to shed tears every morning in the form of dew. Memnon, an Ethiopian, fought for Troy and was killed by Achilles.

Epeius: Famous Greek boxer and craftsman who built the Trojan Horse.

Eurybates: Odysseus' herald.

Furies: (Or Erinyes, known also (to appease them) as 'the kindly ones'). Divine avengers of crime, particularly those against kin.

Glaucus: A Lycian Greek leader on the Trojan side who exchanged golden armour for Diomedes' bronze.

Gorgon: According to the Greek poet Hesiod, there were originally three, the Medusa (killed by Theseus) being only the best known.

Hades: God of the dead and the Underworld (as Zeus was of the sky and Poseidon of the sea).

Hebe: A daughter of Zeus and Hera and handmaid to the other gods.

Hecuba: Wife of Priam and mother of Hector, awarded to Odysseus after the war.

Hector: Son of Priam and greatest hero of the Trojans.

Helen: 'Of Troy' (or Argos), wife of Menelaus, lover of Paris, daughter of Zeus and sister of Agamemnon's wife Clytemnestra.

Helenus: A son of Priam and a Trojan seer.

Hephaestus: Lame craftsman and forge god. Husband of Aphrodite in the *Odyssey*, although not in the *Iliad* where she is Charis (of the shining veil).

Hera: Goddess wife (and sister) of Zeus.

Heracles: Most famous of all legendary Greek heroes and a son of Zeus, performer of the twelve famous labours set by the Athenian king Eristheus. Called Hercules by the Romans.

Hermes: Son of Zeus, messenger of the gods and conductor of souls to the Underworld.

Idomeneus: A Cretan chieftain and one of the Greeks' main leaders.

Iris: A messenger of the gods to men and personification of the rainbow (which, of course, visibly connects heaven and earth).

Jason: Leader of the Argonauts who sailed to Colchis to recover the Golden Fleece.

Leto: A goddess who bore the twin gods Apollo and Artemis to Zeus.

Lycurgus: A legendary king of Thrace who persecuted the god Dionysus and was struck blind or driven mad by him so that he killed his own son.

Machaon: A son of Asclepius, the great Greek physician and son of Apollo, wounded by Paris in the *Iliad*.

Menelaus: King of Sparta, younger brother of Agamemnon and husband of Helen.

Meriones: Nephew of Idomeneus of the Cretans and a leading Greek junior chief.

Myrmidons: Achilles' soldiers, literally the 'ant people'.

Neoptolemus: Son of Achilles.

Nestor: A wordy but respected old Greek chieftain from Pylos on the western coast of the Peloponnese.

Odysseus: Called Ulysses by the Romans, chief of a group of Ionian islands headed by Ithaca.

Oedipus: = 'swollen foot'. A ruler of Thebes who unknowingly killed his father and married his mother. The subject of a famous play (and Freud's even more famous complex).

Olympus: Supposed home of the Greek gods, a mountain in northern Thessaly.

Orpheus: A legendary Greek poet whose lyre playing enchanted even wild animals.

Orion: Legendary hero and hunter from Boeotia (region just north of Athens). Killed by Artemis and turned into the constellation of that name.

Paeon: The healing god.

Pandarus: A Trojan leader and archer who wounded Menelaus and Diomedes and was killed by the latter in Book 5 of the *Iliad*..

Paris: The son of Priam who seduced Helen and so caused the Trojan War. Sometimes called Alexandros.

Patroclus: Closest friend and lieutenant of Achilles, killed by Hector. In childhood he killed his friend, Clysonymus in an argument so that he and his father had to seek refuge with Achilles' father.

Persephone: Goddess wife of Hades and joint-ruler with him of the Underworld.

Philoctetes: A famous but mysterious Greek archer hero (absent from the *Iliad*) marooned on the island of Lemnos after a snake-bite that would not heal.

Phoenix: Achilles' oldest companion and tutor.

Polydamas: Greek fighter and wise counsellor of Hector.

Poseidon: Brother of Zeus, god of the sea and earthquakes (hence the common reference to him as 'Earthshaker'). A supporter of the Greeks.

Priam: King of Troy and reputedly father to over fifty sons.

Sarpedon: A Lycian son of Zeus, greatest of the Trojan allies and comrade of Glaucus (*q.v.*).

Sisyphus: A legendary king of Corinth, famous for his trickery. Condemned after his death to roll a boulder in Hades forever uphill. Only for it to forever roll back again.

Stentor: A famously loud-voiced Greek hero who gave us the word 'stentorian'.

Sthelenus: Charioteer and leader, with Diomedes, of the Greeks of Argos.

Themis: A titan (secondary order of older gods). In Homer, she kept order at assemblies and banquets.

Thersites: A Greek soldier who is a sneering critic of the heroes. Eventually killed by Achilles.

Tethys: Another of the twelve titans, a sea and river goddess.

Thetis: Mother of Achilles. A Nereid, or sea-nymph daughter of Nereus, the 'Old Man of The Sea'.

Xanthus: (Also Scamander) one of the two chief rivers of Troy. Also a god and a son of Zeus.

Zeus: Son of Cronos, greatest of Homer's gods and ultimate determiner (within destiny) of what happens in the Trojan War.

CPSIA information can be obtained
at www.ICGtesting.com
Printed in the USA
LVHW080702230619
622063LV00031B/561/P

9 781533 374080